W9-BIN-039

# MARYLAND

# MARYLAND BY ROAD

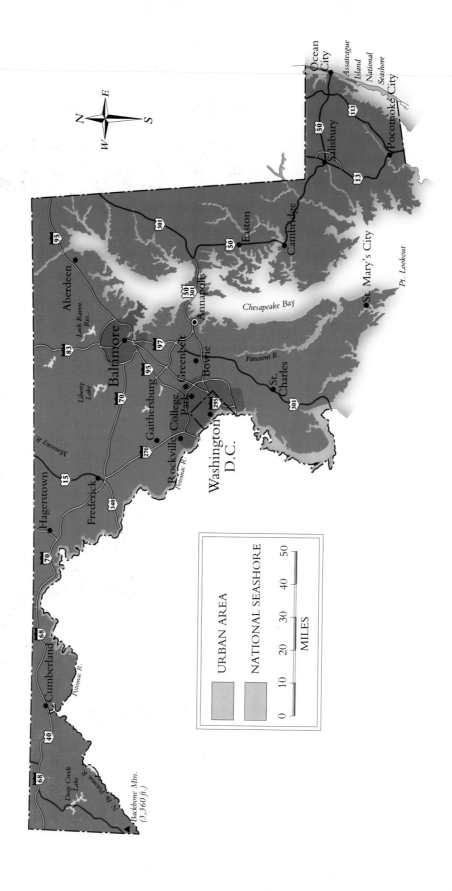

URBAN AREA

NATIONAL SEASHORE

MILES

0  10  20  30  40  50

Ocean City

Assateague Island National Seashore

Pocomoke City

113

Salisbury

50

13

Easton

Cambridge

50

St. Mary's City

Pt. Lookout

Chesapeake Bay

301

95

Aberdeen

Loch Raven Res.

83

97

Baltimore

Greenbelt

Bowie

Patuxent R.

St. Charles

301

95

Liberty Lake

70

Gaithersburg

College Park

295

Rockville

Potomac R.

Washington D.C.

270

Monocacy R.

15

Hagerstown

Frederick

340

70

68

Cumberland

Potomac R.

40

68

Deep Creek Lake

N. Br. Potomac R.

Backbone Mtn. (3,360 ft.)

Annapolis

50
301

N  E  S  W

# CELEBRATE THE STATES
# MARYLAND

## Leslie Rauth

## BENCHMARK BOOKS

MARSHALL CAVENDISH
NEW YORK

Benchmark Books
Marshall Cavendish Corporation
99 White Plains Road
Tarrytown, New York 10591-9001

Copyright © 2000 by Marshall Cavendish Corporation

All rights reserved

Library of Congress Cataloging-in-Publication Data
Rauth, Leslie.
Maryland / Leslie Rauth
p.   cm. — (Celebrate the states)
Includes bibliographical references and index.
Summary: Discusses the geographic features, history, government, people,
and attractions of the state known as "America in Miniature."
ISBN 0-7614-0671-9 (lib. bdg.)
1. Maryland—Juvenile literature. [1. Maryland.] I. Title. II. Series.
F181.3.P54   2000   975.2—dc21   98-43960   CIP   AC

Maps and graphics supplied by Oxford Cartographers, Oxford, England

Photo Research by Candlepants Incorporated

Cover Photo: Photri Inc.

The photographs in this book are used by permission and through the courtesy of; *Photo Researchers, Inc.* :
Lowell Georgia, 6-7, 62; Jeff Lepore, 19; Jim Amos, 25; Vanessa Vick, 60(bottom); Jeanne White, 79; Spencer
Grant, 108; Richard Novitz, 111; Maslowski, 119 (top); Alan Detrick, 119(bottom); Leonard Lee Rue, 122
(top); Tom McHugh, 122(bottom); Jerry Wachter, 136. *Maryland Historical Society, Baltimore, Maryland:*
30-31, 35, 37, 39, 41, 42, 46, 47(top and bottom), 92. ©*Enoch Pratt Free Library:* 33.*Heather R. Davidson :*
10-11, 17, 60(top), 82. *Photri Inc.* : Mike Boroff, 13, 16; 59, 76, 104, 110. *Dan Beigel* : 14, 20, 22, 23, 50-51,
64, 66-67, 69, 71, 73, 75, 83, 84-85, 113, 115, 117, 125, back cover. *Skip Willits Marketing* : 28, 103. *Corbis/*
Paul A. Souders: 55; Kurt Krieger, 89; Bettmann: 87(right), 97, 129, 131(bottom), 133; UPI: 87(left), 128,
131(top), 132, 134, 135; Agence France Presse: 94.*Corbis:* 95.   *Archive Photos:* 88, 98. *Archive Photos:* Frank
Driggs Collection, 90; Victor Malafronte/Archive News Photos, 91. *Annapolis & Anne Arundel County
Conference & Visitors Bureau* : 80. *Image Bank* : Kay Chernush, 100-101. *Stuart Haman* : 107. *Office of the
Secretary of State of Maryland*: 118(bottom).

Printed in Italy

3   5   6   4   2

# CONTENTS

# MARYLAND IS . . .

**Maryland is a land of vast beauty . . .**

Maryland "is bathed in a singular and various beauty, from the stately estuaries of the Chesapeake to the peaks of the Blue Ridge."
—writer H. L. Mencken, 1922

"This baye is the most delightfull water I ever saw."
—Father Andrew White upon arriving in 1634

**. . . and magnificent waters . . .**

"The Chesapeake! . . . This was the magical place where the waters became wider than those of the Susquehanna, where storms of enormous magnitude churned up waves of frightening power. This was the river of rivers, where the fish wore precious shells."
—author James Michener

**. . . which Marylanders appreciate deeply.**

"We have a distinctive way of life down here [on the Eastern Shore], a good life that is rich in many things."
—former governor J. Millard Tawes

**Maryland is filled with unexpected places . . .**

"One Marylander's place is so different from another's. Maryland is no artful mosaic, no tapestry of fabrics carefully woven into a whole. It is more a kaleidoscope, bits and pieces thrown together."
—author Eugene L. Meyer

"Baltimore is a city of . . . neighbors sharing steamed crabs in the back yard, and downtown waitresses who call their customers Hon."　　　　　　　　　—newspaper columnist Michael Olesker

## . . . and interesting people.

"When it comes to eating muskrat, that's when we separate real Eastern Shoremen from everyone else."　　　—Eastern Shore cook

"Maryland don't want us, West Virginia won't have us, and we don't want Pennsylvania. We want a state of our own."
　　　　　　　　　　　　　　　—Garrett County citizen

---

Maryland has some of everything—mountains, valleys, beaches, cities, suburbs, farms, and quiet country towns. Maryland started as a colony founded on religious tolerance. Today, its citizens have come from all over the world. The spectacular Chesapeake Bay is only one of Maryland's treasures. You might think you know Maryland, but this state will find ways to surprise you.

# 1

# AMERICA IN
# MINIATURE

**O**nly eight states are smaller than Maryland. Yet within Maryland's borders is a wide variety of landscape, plants, and animals. No wonder people refer to Maryland as America in Miniature.

Maryland is bordered by Virginia and the District of Columbia to the south; West Virginia to the west; Pennsylvania to the north; and Delaware to the east. Thirty-one miles of Atlantic Ocean shoreline also form Maryland's eastern border. The state is shaped like no other: it has been described as a gun with the muzzle pointing west.

## THE MOUNTAINOUS WEST

The western corner of Maryland is very mountainous and covered with forest. According to journalist Eugene L. Meyer, it is "a land of splendid scenery, of Appalachian ridges and high meadows." The region's deep forests provide a pleasant retreat from more populated areas. "The mountains are aflame in autumn and serene in summer," Meyer once wrote.

The state's highest point is here, in the Allegheny Mountains: Backbone Mountain is 3,360 feet high. (Though that may sound big, the highest point in the United States is Alaska's Mount McKinley at 20,320 feet.) The narrowest part of the state is located at the town of Hancock where it's less than two miles border-to-border.

*The Potomac River forms Maryland's southern border and flows into the Chesapeake Bay.*

East of the Allegheny Mountains is a series of valleys with very fertile soil. Grain is grown here on picturesque farms, and there are a lot of apple orchards. Marble and limestone come from this region, including the marble that was used to build most of the Washington Monument in Washington, D.C.

Farther east rise the Blue Ridge Mountains, one of the loveliest areas of Maryland, where waves of forested mountains meet the sky. On bright days, a blue haze seems to hover in the distance, giving the mountains their name.

## PIEDMONT PLATEAU

Past the mountains, the land slopes into rolling hills called the Piedmont Plateau. Farms growing wheat, corn, oats, and other

*It may seem surprising that Maryland has so many horse farms. Yet horse racing is very popular in Maryland. The Preakness, one of racing's prestigious Triple Crown events, is held each year at Baltimore's Pimlico Race Course.*

crops dot the landscape. Horse farms are also common in the Piedmont. Twice as many thoroughbred horses are raised here per square mile as in Kentucky.

The Piedmont Plateau comes to a dramatic end. The altitude drops, and the rivers and streams that had been flowing gently through the hills suddenly cascade quickly to the plains below, often creating waterfalls. This point where the Piedmont Plateau ends and the Atlantic Coastal Plain begins is called the Fall Line. Historically, boats couldn't travel any farther up the river than the Fall Line, so a town was built. Baltimore is at the Fall Line.

One of the Fall Line's most remarkable waterfalls is Great Falls on the Potomac River. Only fifteen miles northwest of Washington, D.C., this raging white water is a popular site for picnickers and hikers looking to escape the city for an afternoon. "Great Falls's fearsome beauty is incredible, but you do have to be careful" because of its dangerous currents, says native Marylander Cindy Herrle.

## ATLANTIC COASTAL PLAIN

More than half of Maryland is part of the Atlantic Coastal Plain, which stretches from New Jersey to Florida. Maryland's portion is cut into two sections by the Chesapeake Bay: the low-lying Eastern Shore and the higher ground of the Western Shore. The Eastern Shore is part of a peninsula shared by three states—Delaware, Maryland, and Virginia—which is sometimes referred to as the Delmarva Peninsula. The Eastern Shore is filled with marshy wetlands. The sky looms high overhead; few trees break up the

*In 1608, explorer John Smith called Maryland the "Delightsome Land."
Few would disagree today.*

flatness. Produce and poultry farms stretch out alongside roads, and every back road seems to lead to a marsh, a creek, the bay, or the ocean. The Western Shore is similar though more forested.

*Muddy Creek Falls, in Swallow State Park, is one of the highest waterfalls in Maryland at sixty-three feet.*

## RIVERS

Most of Maryland's rivers flow into the Chesapeake Bay. The Potomac is Maryland's longest river, winding for 285 miles along the state's southern border before spilling into the bay. The East Coast's biggest river is the Susquehanna, which starts in New York, travels through Pennsylvania and Maryland, and then empties into the Chesapeake Bay. Other important rivers on the Western Shore are the Severn, Gunpowder, Patapsco, and Patuxent. On the Eastern Shore, the Chester, Choptank, and Pocomoke Rivers flow into the bay.

In western Maryland, a twenty-one-mile segment of the Youghiogheny River (known as the Yock) has been designated Maryland's first "Wild River." Thanks to the Yock's remote and rugged character, some threatened or endangered plants and animals that are no longer found elsewhere still survive there. To maintain the unique beauty of the Yock, logging and development are limited around it. The Yock and the surrounding areas are ideal for trout fishing, white-water rafting, and hiking.

## PLANTS AND ANIMALS

About 30 percent of Maryland is covered with trees; most of the forests are found in western Maryland and the Piedmont. Spruce, hemlock, white pine, maple, and hickory trees are particularly plentiful. Yellow pine, cedar, and red gum trees grow in southern Maryland. The wetlands along the Chesapeake Bay have cypress trees. The oldest tree in Maryland is said to be the Wye Oak in Talbot County, which is more than 450 years old and 31 feet around.

Nine hundred different species of animals call Maryland home. Deer abound throughout the state, and red and gray foxes, raccoons, squirrels, opossums, skunks, woodchucks, weasels, and cottontail rabbits live in the forests. A few bears remain in the mountainous regions of the state. The Delmarva fox squirrel, an endangered species, lives in the Eastern Shore. Wild ponies roam Assateague Island, a barrier island in the Atlantic Ocean. Legend has it that the ponies are descended from a sixteenth-century herd that swam ashore off a sinking Spanish ship. But most likely, the ponies escaped from herds that grazed on the island.

*The Delmarva fox squirrel, an endangered species, can be found in four Eastern Shore counties.*

*Wild ponies on Assateague Island survive by eating seaweed and shore grass.*

Early settlers were amazed by the number of ducks and other birds in Maryland. In 1680, two Dutchmen named Jaspar Danckaerts and Peter Sluyter kept a journal of their trip through Maryland. When they reached the Susquehanna River, they wrote, "The water was so black with [ducks] . . . when they flew up there was a rushing and vibration of the air like a great storm coming through the trees, even like the rumbling of distant thunder."

There are still lots of birds in Maryland. Some live in the state, some spend the winter, and some just pass through. Forty-one types of ducks have been observed in Maryland, including mallards, black ducks, canvasbacks, wood ducks, and northern pintails. Birds that winter in Maryland include Canada and snow geese and tundra swans. Other Maryland shorebirds are great blue herons, sandpipers, plovers, gulls, and terns.

Away from the water, Marylanders enjoy watching cardinals, bluebirds, wrens, doves, mockingbirds, and many other types of songbirds. Hawks wheel overhead, and there are several nesting areas for bald eagles throughout the state, including the Blackwater National Wildlife Refuge and Calvert Cliffs State Park. The state bird is the Baltimore oriole, named after Lord Baltimore. He chose orange and black as the colors of his coat of arms because he admired the vibrant bird.

The Chesapeake Bay is filled with more than two hundred varieties of fish. Even more than fish, the bay is known for its shellfish. In fact, *Chesapeake* comes from a Native American word meaning "great shellfish bay." Maryland is so proud of its reputation as a source of shellfish that it even has an official state crustacean— the Maryland blue crab. Maryland writer Tom Horton once remarked, "We love our crabs in Chesapeake country—love to eat them steamed and fried, in crabcakes and stuffed into flounder and striped bass fillets." The Chesapeake provides 50 percent of the nation's blue crab harvest.

## CLIMATE

Like many other aspects of Maryland, the state's climate has some of everything. Eastern Maryland enjoys mild winters, though the summers can be quite warm and humid. Western Maryland is colder and snowy, as would be expected in a more mountainous

*Maryland's famous blue crab. The male crab is called a "jimmy" and the female is called a "sook" or "sooky."*

area. Garrett County has an average annual snowfall of one hundred inches, versus just eight to ten inches on the Eastern Shore. Summers in the mountains are delightfully cool. Occasionally, hurricanes or small tornadoes will hit Maryland, but in general, nothing worse than a thunderstorm or snowstorm strikes the state.

## A DELICATE BALANCE

"The Bay. There is no possible confusion with any other body of water, no need for more precise description," wrote William W. Warner in his award-winning book *Beautiful Swimmers*. Indeed, nothing defines Maryland like the Chesapeake Bay. It's what people think of first when they think of the state.

While the entire bay is only two hundred miles long, in Maryland it has four thousand miles of shoreline. At first glance the bay may not seem very dramatic. "Physically, the Chesapeake estuary is

*Maryland's average annual snowfall is twenty-seven inches, but an average of one hundred inches falls annually in Garrett County in western Maryland.*

## PFIESTERIA HYSTERIA

In the autumn of 1996, fishermen along the Pocomoke River noticed something alarming—fish with lesions, or open sores, along their bodies. The following year, thousands of fish in this river died. Again, the fish had red sores on their bodies. What was worse, many people who handled these fish suddenly suffered short-term memory loss, nausea, rashes, and eye irritations.

The fish were afflicted by *Pfiesteria piscicida*, a toxic microbe. Maryland governor Parris Glendening quickly closed the river to swimming, fishing, and boating. He also asked a commission of experts to study the problem.

The governor's decision was controversial. Many thought he was overreacting and alarming people needlessly. Sales of Maryland seafood plummeted. But the governor stood his ground, saying, "We could not delay the announcement of the health risk. What if one family went out water-skiing and were seriously affected?"

The commission reported that chicken manure, which is used as fertilizer, was polluting the river. During rainstorms, runoff from the farms where the manure had been used ended up in the river. Now the state is working with farmers to find a solution to this vexing problem.

John R. Griffin, secretary of the Maryland Department of Natural Resources, called the fish kill "a little alarm bell that we've got to be even more vigilant in our efforts" to keep the environment clean.

among the gentlest bodies of water of its size, lacking furious currents, rocky shoals, mammoth waves, or even much of a daily tidal drop," says environmental writer Tom Horton. It's the special combination of all its parts that makes the bay so beloved by Marylanders. In Baltimore's busy Inner Harbor tourist area, people step aside from the bustle to stare down at the rippling water, gaze out beyond the lights, ponder where those ripples could carry them. The same bay also includes a series of intricate Eastern Shore creeks and marshes clogged with thick grasses. There, the sounds are birds calling to one another and the lapping of gently moving water.

When Marylander Cindy Herrle talks about the bay, it's as if

*Watermen dredging oysters from their skipjack. Another method of retrieving oysters is by tonging, using large metal tongs with teeth like a comb to pull oysters from the bottom of the bay.*

# LAND AND WATER

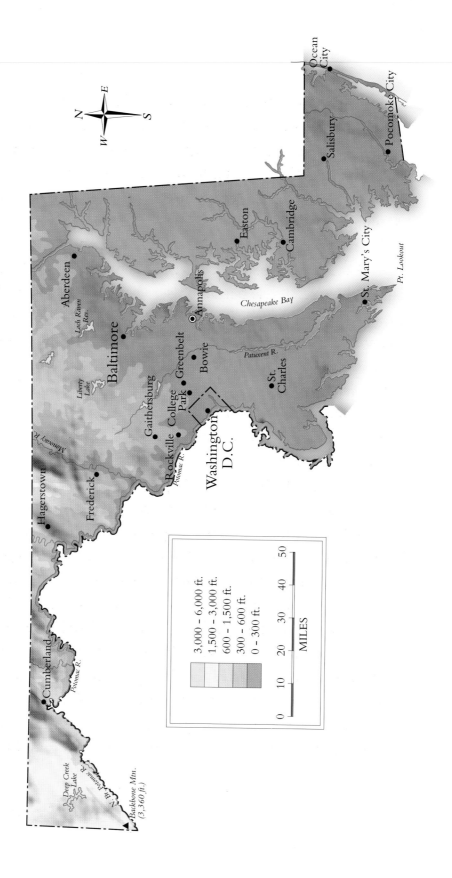

N
E
S
W

Ocean City

Poconoke City

Salisbury

Cambridge

Easton

St. Mary's City

Pt. Lookout

Chesapeake Bay

Aberdeen

Loch Raven Res.

Baltimore

Annapolis

Liberty Lake

Bowie

Patuxent R.

Greenbelt

St. Charles

Gaithersburg

College Park

Rockville

Monocacy R.

Potomac R.

Washington D.C.

Hagerstown

Frederick

Cumberland

Potomac R.

Deep Creek Lake

N. Br. Potomac R.

Backbone Mtn. (3,360 ft.)

3,000 - 6,000 ft.
1,500 - 3,000 ft.
600 - 1,500 ft.
300 - 600 ft.
0 - 300 ft.

0    10    20    30    40    50

MILES

she's describing a person: "The bay has multiple personalities—some days it's very calm and peaceful, and some days it's very angry. When it's angry, whitecaps crowd the surface, and waves can reach five or six feet. It's fairly moody. Some days the water is flat and calm in the morning, by afternoon it's rough, and then by evening, everything's all smoothed out again."

The bay was created at the end of the last Ice Age, between 12,000 and 18,000 years ago. As glaciers retreated and the polar ice caps melted, sea levels began to rise. The rising ocean engulfed the coast and flooded the Susquehanna River valley, creating the bay. Today, the bay's average depth is only 21 feet, though its deepest point is 170 feet.

Maryland's top environmental concern is the health of the bay. It is the nation's largest estuary—a combination of salty ocean water and freshwater from rivers, tides, and rain. A delicate balance is needed to sustain the 2,700 species of oysters, crabs, fish, and other living things that call the bay home.

For at least twenty years, Marylanders have realized their bay was in trouble. Pollution has been taking its toll. Rivers that feed into the bay pass through areas with lots of farms. Some of the fertilizer used by farmers and the nutrient-rich manure produced by cattle end up in the rivers, which flow into the bay. The result? Too many nutrients upset the bay's delicate balance. Certain plants such as floating algae thrive on these fertilizers and nutrients, choking out the light and oxygen needed by the underwater plants that ducks, geese, and swans feed on and in which crabs hide.

In 1997, the federal and state governments agreed to pay Maryland farmers as much as $200 million to take 100,000 acres of

*People worry that building too many houses near the bay will destroy fragile marshlands.*

farmland out of production and plant trees and grasses as buffers against the pollution running into the bay. Farmer Paul Crowl said, "It sounds like a good program—good for farmers and good for water quality." Studies show that forest buffers can remove some of the nutrients in the water that passes through them.

Too many people living near the bay is also a problem. More than 2.3 million people live within twenty miles of the bay and its tributaries. Building houses near the water often destroys protective grasses, forests, and wetlands. "Managing growth is absolutely the toughest challenge we face," said an official with the Chesapeake Bay Foundation. Maryland has begun to restrict development along most of the remaining shoreline, requiring a thousand-foot buffer zone around the bay and its tidal rivers. Yet people keep coming. Several counties near the bay are among Maryland's fastest growing, and the impact of these new people remains to be seen.

In the 1980s, vast quantities of oysters in the bay were wiped out by disease. Oysters help maintain the bay's delicate balance, filtering out excess algae and silt as they take water through their system. At one time, there were enough oysters to filter the water of the entire bay every week or two. Now it takes nearly a year. In an effort to rebuild the oyster population, restrictions have been placed on how many oysters can be harvested from the bay. Baby oysters are also being grown in hatcheries and then introduced into the bay. Though the number of oysters in the bay has increased moderately, some people wonder if these measures came too late. "How did we let such treasure almost slip away?" asked writer Tom Horton. "Nothing in my native Maryland is more sacred than the Bay."

# 2 A FOUNDATION OF TOLERANCE

**P**eople first came to Maryland at least 10,000 years ago. Archaeologists have discovered the stone tips of spears used by these prehistoric men and women.

## NATIVE AMERICANS

As time passed, the people living in the area became the Indian tribes encountered by the first colonists arriving from England. On the Eastern Shore were the Nanticokes, Choptanks, Pocomokes, and Wicomicos. The Piscataway and Patuxent tribes lived on the Western Shore. These tribes all spoke variations of the Algonquian language. To the north, where the Susquehanna River meets the Chesapeake Bay, lived the Susquehannocks. This tribe sometimes attacked its more peaceful neighbors to the south.

The Chesapeake Bay region provided plenty of food for the Indians. Men hunted and trapped bears, deer, and wild turkeys. They hollowed out tree trunks to make canoes and went fishing with nets and spears. Women grew corn, beans, and squash and gathered clams, oysters, nuts, and strawberries. The Indians lived in villages of huts made from branches and bark, often surrounded by wooden fences called palisades.

Englishman John Smith, of the Jamestown settlement in Virginia, sailed up the Chesapeake Bay in 1608 and explored the region thoroughly. He took the news back to Virginia that Maryland was a good place to settle and that it had lots of opportunities for trading tools and cloth to the Indians in exchange for valuable furs. Many men in Virginia believed Smith, and soon they were traveling to Maryland.

## LORD BALTIMORE'S DREAM

Meanwhile, in England, Sir George Calvert asked King Charles I to give him land to found a colony in Maryland. Calvert, who was

*Sir George Calvert founded Maryland as a colony of religious tolerance. Sadly, he died in England without ever setting foot in Maryland.*

the lord of the English province of Baltimore, did not belong to the Church of England, as most English did. He was Roman Catholic, and at that time, Catholics were persecuted by the English government. Calvert's dream was to found a colony in the New World where people of different religious faiths would no longer suffer persecution. Charles agreed to Calvert's request in 1632—two months after George Calvert had died. So the king granted the official charter to Calvert's son, Cecil Calvert, the second Lord Baltimore.

In 1634, two ships, the *Ark* and the *Dove*, brought about 150 people, both Protestant and Catholic, to the new land. The colonists reached St. Clement's Island in the Potomac River, and on March 25, 1634, the priests traveling with them held the first-ever Catholic Mass in Maryland. After several weeks of exploring, the newcomers found a small inlet on the western side of the bay. They called their settlement St. Marys (now known as St. Mary's City). The Indians were helpful to the colonists, hoping to gain protection from the dreaded Susquehannocks.

The new Marylanders started farming their lands, growing wheat, corn, and tobacco. Tobacco was especially profitable, and soon farmers established tobacco plantations, huge, family-owned estates that required many workers. At first this work was done by indentured servants, poor people whose passage from England to Maryland had been paid for by wealthy colonists. In return, the indentured servants were required to work about four years. But by 1700, African slaves were working the plantations.

More and more colonists were coming to Maryland, taking over land that had been used by the Native Americans. Some of the

*The* Ark *and the* Dove *landed at St. Clement's Island, and colonists went ashore on March 25, 1634. March 25 is still celebrated as Maryland Day.*

tribes fought to keep their lands, but they couldn't win. European diseases such as smallpox took a toll on the native population. Eventually no Native American tribes remained in Maryland.

The once mighty Susquehannocks were pushed from place to place. In 1763, the last twenty members of the tribe were murdered by a Pennsylvania mob, eliminating the tribe altogether. Even today, only about half of Maryland's small Native American population is descended from the region's original tribes. The others are descendants of tribes that came to Maryland from other places after colonial times.

During the eighteenth century, a dispute raged between Pennsylvania and Maryland over their border. Two surveyors were hired to settle the matter. Charles Mason and Jeremiah Dixon completed their work in 1767, and the line they drew became known as the Mason-Dixon Line. This border not only separates Maryland from Pennsylvania but also is considered the dividing line between the North and South.

## THE AMERICAN REVOLUTION

In the mid-eighteenth century, England and France fought a war over control of their colonies in North America. At the war's end in 1763, England emerged as the sole master of the American colonies. But the war had been so long and costly that the British Parliament decided to impose new taxes on the colonists. One of the first was the Stamp Act of 1765. Under this law, colonists were required to buy special tax stamps whenever they bought newspapers and legal documents. This tax was very unpopular throughout America. After many protests, the tax was repealed. This was just the first of many conflicts between the colonies and Great Britain that led to the Revolutionary War and, eventually, America's independence.

Though no Revolutionary War battles occurred in Maryland, more than 23,000 Marylanders fought for independence. During the Battle of Long Island, Maryland soldiers proved their bravery by holding off the British so other American troops could make their way to safety. General George Washington said, "No troops poured out their blood more freely for the common cause than those of

Maryland." Those Maryland soldiers, whom Washington called "troops of the line," gave Maryland one of its nicknames—the Old Line State.

The official end of the Revolutionary War came in 1784 when the Treaty of Paris was signed in Annapolis at the Maryland State House. Maryland became the seventh state of the new country four years later when it ratified the U.S. Constitution. In 1791, Maryland (along with Virginia) donated land on the Potomac River so the young nation could build a permanent capital city, Washington, D.C.

*Baltimore in 1796. The first census in 1790 counted 13,500 people living in Baltimore—making it the fourth-largest city in the new country, behind Philadelphia, New York, and Boston.*

## BUILDING A NEW COUNTRY

By this time Baltimore had become Maryland's major port and the largest city south of the Mason-Dixon Line. In the whole country, only New York, Philadelphia, and Boston were larger. It seemed that the United States was off to a fine beginning, trading goods with many other countries. However, the British didn't like having to compete against the American shipping trade, so tensions grew between the two nations, and eventually President James Madison declared war.

Maryland played a central role in the War of 1812. The British wanted to capture the port of Baltimore because it was an important trade center. In 1814, British ships attacked Fort McHenry in the Battle of Baltimore. James Ellicott, who observed the scene, wrote, "The bombardment of the fort was a scene interesting; terrible and grand. During the whole of last night we were able from the tops of the houses in town to trace every rocket and shell from the time it left the mortar until it struck or exploded in the air."

Another Marylander watching this attack was Francis Scott Key, who was a prisoner on a British ship in the harbor. As the British released more and more bombs, the sky filled with smoke and night fell, so Key could no longer see the American flag above Fort McHenry. The next morning, when he saw the American flag still waving high above the fort, he scribbled words of relief on the back of an envelope. These words were the poem that became "The Star-Spangled Banner," our national anthem.

After the war ended, the country turned to solving other problems, including improving transportation. In 1824, work began

*The British bombardment of Fort McHenry inspired Francis Scott Key to write "The Star-Spangled Banner," a poem that later became our national anthem.*

on the Chesapeake and Delaware Canal, a waterway that provided ships a shortcut between Baltimore and the Atlantic Ocean. And in 1828, construction started on the Chesapeake and Ohio Canal in an effort to link Washington, D.C., and the Potomac River with the Ohio River valley. Though the canal was never finished, by 1850 it reached western Maryland.

Even more important than the canals was the railroad. In 1830, the Baltimore and Ohio Railroad began offering the nation's first passenger rail service, between Ellicotts' Mills and Baltimore. The steam-powered locomotives went twenty miles an hour—unheard of at the time!

## A DIVIDED NATION

As the young country grew, people began to have different views regarding slavery. While it was declared illegal in all the Northern states in 1804, the Southern states refused to yield to pressure to outlaw slavery. Maryland was in the middle of this increasingly bitter fight. Baltimorean McHenry Howard wrote to a friend, "I live just between the North and the South, hearing both sides of the question and *feeling* both sides."

The disagreement over slavery erupted into civil war in April 1861, after some Southern states seceded from the Union and formed the Confederate States of America. Though Maryland was located south of the Mason-Dixon Line, it did not secede. President Abraham Lincoln sent Union troops into Maryland to prevent secession because he did not want Washington, D.C., totally surrounded by Confederate states.

Yet some Marylanders were still torn about which side to support. Many farmers in western Maryland and the Piedmont did not favor slavery. But the tobacco planters wanted slaves to work on their big plantations. It's believed that 20,000 Marylanders joined the Confederate army during the course of the war, and in many areas—particularly the Eastern Shore—citizens sided with the South. Many Marylanders who fought for the Union joined regiments dedicated to guarding Maryland rather than invading the South. Approximately 25,000 Maryland men joined the Union army, and an additional 5,000 served as sailors and marines.

Maryland was the site of one of the worst battles in the Civil War, the Battle of Antietam, in 1862. More than 23,000 Union and

# THE UNDERGROUND RAILROAD'S GREATEST CONDUCTOR

During the nineteenth century, many people decided they could not sit idly by and tolerate slavery. The Underground Railroad helped slaves make their way to safety and freedom in the North and Canada by following a route of safe havens. Free African Americans and sympathetic whites guided the runaway slaves from one place to the next, at great risk to their own safety.

Harriet Tubman, who was born into slavery on an Eastern Shore plantation, was one of the most famous "conductors" of the Underground Railroad. When she was almost thirty years old, she had escaped to the North, assisted by the Underground Railroad in a slow house-to-house journey from Maryland to Delaware to freedom in Pennsylvania. "When I found I had crossed that [Mason-Dixon] line . . . the sun came like gold through the trees, and over the fields, and I felt like I was in Heaven," she said. She vowed she would return for the people she'd had to leave behind. Tubman returned to Maryland nineteen times to lead approximately three hundred slaves to freedom. She said, "On my Underground Railroad I never ran my train off the track and I never lost a passenger."

At one point, plantation owners offered a $40,000 reward for her capture—far more than the fees of $25 to $150 that were normal for returning a runaway slave. Thanks to Tubman's heroism, members of her family—as well as many other strangers—were able to live out their lives in freedom.

*Burnside Bridge at the Battle of Antietam in the Civil War. For almost four hours, Union general Ambrose Burnside's troops were prevented from crossing this bridge, kept at bay by only four hundred Georgia riflemen.*

Confederate soldiers were killed in a single day near Sharpsburg, in western Maryland. James H. Rigby, a Confederate soldier, described the battle: "The crying of the wounded for water, the shrieks of the dying, mingled with the screeching of the shells, made up a scene so truly appalling and horrible that I hoped to God, that I might never witness such another."

The Civil War ended on April 9, 1865. Five days later, Marylander John Wilkes Booth killed President Lincoln in Washington, D.C. Booth escaped back to Maryland before being caught in Virginia.

## MARYLAND GROWS

After the war, Baltimore grew rapidly, with its population nearly doubling between 1870 and 1900. The new Baltimoreans came both from rural parts of the United States and from many European nations, including Germany, Ireland, Russia, and Poland.

In 1917, the United States entered World War I, and more than 60,000 Marylanders served in the military. Maryland contributed to the war effort by building ships and producing such necessities as canned food. After the war, Maryland's economy continued to grow until the Great Depression swept the nation in the early 1930s. More than half of Maryland's factories closed or cut production during the Depression. World War II lifted the country

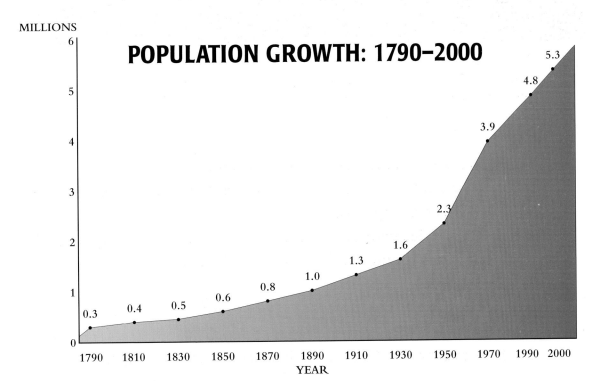

POPULATION GROWTH: 1790–2000

# BALTIMORE FIRE

On February 7 and 8, 1904, a tremendous fire wiped out practically the entire downtown section of Baltimore. Jones Falls, referred to in the song as "silver falls," was one of the points at which the firemen stopped the advance of the blaze.

WALKERTON ELEMENTARY SCHOOL LIBRARY

*Chorus*

Fire, fire, I heard the cry, From ev - 'ry breeze. that
Strong men in an - guish prayed, Call - ing out— to

passed me by. All the world— was one sad cry of—
heav'n for aid, While the fire— in ru - in laid Fair—

pi - ty,— Bal - ti - more, the beau - ti - ful cit - y.—

*In the 1880s, immigrants from Europe flocked to the United States, many by way of Baltimore. Only New York City processed more immigrants than Baltimore.*

out of the Depression, and again, Maryland's factories contributed to the war effort, producing ships, nails, cargo planes, bombers, and more.

Back home, Maryland was facing another challenging battle: the issue of civil rights, or equal treatment under the law for Americans of all races. In 1935, Donald Murray had not been permitted to enroll in the University of Maryland School of Law because he was black. Thurgood Marshall, an African-American lawyer, took the

Here is how one observer described oyster shucking at a packing house: "She seizes an oyster, inserts the thin knife between the shells, and with a quick turn of the wrist the shell is opened, the oyster cut loose and dropped into the pan, all with one movement."

In World War II, Maryland continued its tradition as a shipbuilding center.

# TEN LARGEST CITIES

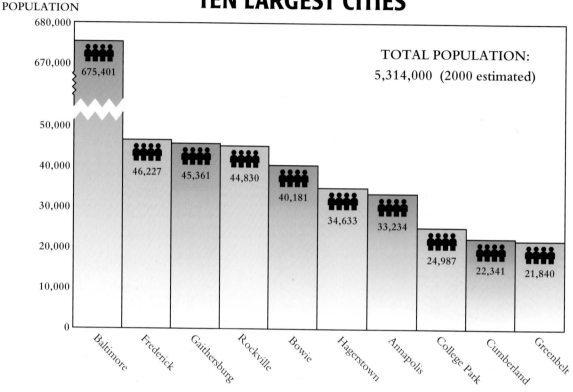

POPULATION

TOTAL POPULATION:
5,314,000 (2000 estimated)

- Baltimore: 675,401
- Frederick: 46,227
- Gaithersburg: 45,361
- Rockville: 44,830
- Bowie: 40,181
- Hagerstown: 34,633
- Annapolis: 33,234
- College Park: 24,987
- Cumberland: 22,341
- Greenbelt: 21,840

case to court and won. Murray became the first African-American student to enter a professional school at a state university south of the Mason-Dixon Line. That was just the beginning of a distinguished career for Thurgood Marshall, who eventually became the first African American to serve on the U.S. Supreme Court.

The 1950s and 1960s brought many changes in Maryland's cities, especially Baltimore. More affluent families began moving out of the cities into brand new communities called suburbs, which featured bigger houses and yards. Cities like Baltimore were left with a population made up primarily of poorer citizens. While this was happening, many factories also cut back on production, so fewer jobs were available.

Maryland boldly rose to face this challenge. To rejuvenate downtown Baltimore, the city built Charles Center, a hotel-office-entertainment complex covering twenty-two acres downtown, which was completed in the late 1960s. Then, in 1980, Harborplace opened on the site of what had once been decaying wharves. This complex of shops and restaurants attracted tourists and new businesses to the city. The area continues to develop, with the addition of the National Aquarium, Oriole Park at Camden Yards, and many more hotels, restaurants, and attractions.

While this renovation of Baltimore has brought more money into the city, vast areas remain stricken with poverty. Some people wonder if all the new development wasn't just "window dressing" that ignored the real problems of the city: crime, poor schools, lack of good-paying jobs. "They had to start somewhere," said resident Kristy Doty. "But there are still plenty of problems facing the city."

But Maryland is a state that faces challenges head-on. From its foundation of religious tolerance, Maryland continues to find ways to ensure that its residents can live together in peace and prosperity.

# 3 GROWING AND CHANGING

*The capitol in Annapolis*

**M**aryland has had four constitutions over the course of its history. The first was adopted during the Revolutionary War in 1776. The fourth and present constitution was adopted in 1867.

## INSIDE GOVERNMENT

Like the federal government, Maryland's government is divided into three branches: executive, legislative, and judicial. A series of checks and balances ensure that no one branch becomes overly powerful.

**Executive.** The executive branch implements and enforces Maryland's laws. The head of this branch—and of the state government as a whole—is the governor, who is elected to a four-year term. Among the governor's responsibilities are presenting the annual state budget to the legislature and appointing people to important positions within the executive and judicial branches.

The governor is assisted by the lieutenant governor, who is elected on a joint ballot with the governor. That means both the governor and the lieutenant governor must be from the same political party. In the event that the governor dies or becomes too ill to serve, the lieutenant governor takes over. Other executive branch officers are the comptroller of the treasury, who oversees financial affairs, and the attorney general, the state's legal adviser.

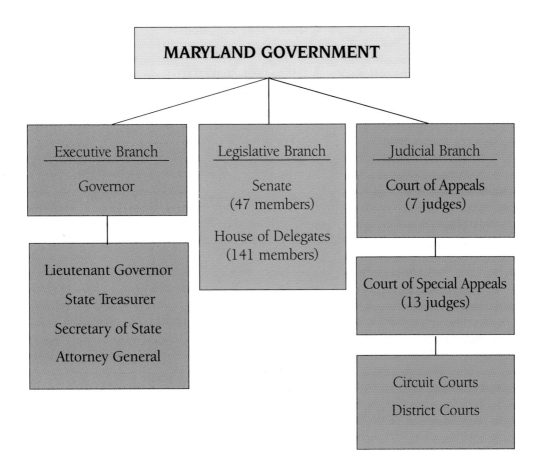

**MARYLAND GOVERNMENT**

**Executive Branch**

Governor

Lieutenant Governor

State Treasurer

Secretary of State

Attorney General

**Legislative Branch**

Senate
(47 members)

House of Delegates
(141 members)

**Judicial Branch**

Court of Appeals
(7 judges)

Court of Special Appeals
(13 judges)

Circuit Courts

District Courts

**Legislative.** The legislative branch is made up of the General Assembly, which consists of the 141-member House of Delegates and the 47-member Senate. The term for all legislators is four years. A bill may be introduced in either house. Once it has passed both houses and has been signed by the governor, it becomes law.

**Judicial.** This judicial branch interprets laws and tries legal cases. Maryland's court system has four levels: the District Court of Maryland (the lowest court); the circuit courts; the Court of Special Appeals; and the Court of Appeals, which is Maryland's highest court. This court of seven judges reviews important cases when the decisions must be based on interpretation of the Maryland Constitution. In general, the governor appoints judges to the four courts, and in some cases (including the Court of Appeals), the appointed judges must be approved by the voters after their term has started.

## SMART GROWTH

In recent years, many Marylanders have become concerned about suburban sprawl, the building of houses farther and farther from the city center. This destroys productive farmland, woodlands and wetlands disappear, and downtowns become abandoned waste-lands. In 1997, Governor Parris Glendening proposed a program creating "Smart Growth Areas." "It is up to you and me to preserve for our children what is best about Maryland—the Chesa-

## GROSS STATE PRODUCT: $155.5 BILLION

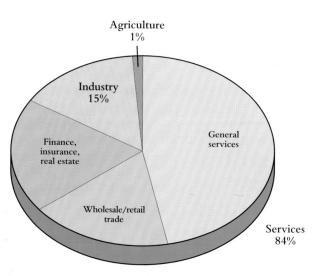

Agriculture 1%

Industry 15%

Finance, insurance, real estate

General services

Wholesale/retail trade

Services 84%

**(2000 estimate)**

# BALTIMORE'S INNOVATIVE MAYOR

Baltimore elected its first African-American mayor on November 3, 1987. Kurt L. Schmoke was born in Baltimore and attended public schools before going on to such prestigious colleges as Yale and Oxford University in England, where he was a Rhodes Scholar. He then earned his law degree at Harvard. After working with President Jimmy Carter's domestic policy staff, he returned to Baltimore, eventually being elected state's attorney, the city's chief prosecutor, where he remained until taking over as mayor.

During his three terms in office, Mayor Schmoke developed a reputation as one of the most innovative mayors in the nation. He tackled Baltimore's problems with energy and new ideas. Shortly after becoming mayor, he attacked the problem of illiteracy by declaring Baltimore "The City That Reads." It was more than a catchy slogan. The mayor established a high-level city agency devoted to literacy and started a private foundation to fund and expand literacy programs throughout the city.

As mayor, Schmoke was unafraid to try new approaches to old problems. He supported a policy that viewed drug abuse as a public health problem, not a law enforcement issue (similar to the way alcoholism or cigarette smoking are health problems). He also suggested legalizing or decriminalizing drugs, making him a controversial—yet always interesting—figure.

peake Bay, our agricultural heritage, our green fields and our open spaces," he said.

The General Assembly then passed several bills, which emphasize conserving and reviving existing communities rather than building outward and creating more sprawl. For example, industries are offered incentives to locate on abandoned factory land in the city rather than putting up whole new buildings in the suburbs. The new laws also offer lower taxes to companies that locate in designated Smart Growth Areas and hire local workers. Governor Glendening says, "Economic growth is vital to a strong economy. *How* we grow is critical."

## GAMBLING

Another issue that has been on the minds of many Marylanders is whether to allow gambling. While polls show Maryland voters favoring slot machines at racetracks by a slim margin, Governor Glendening has vowed "no slots, no casinos, no exceptions" as long as he's in office. Meanwhile, casino owners and gambling interests push to open up Maryland. "As more and more Maryland dollars flow out of state to Delaware and soon to be West Virginia [where slot machines are legal], more and more Marylanders will support slots," predicts Joe DeFrancis, a racetrack owner.

While there are potential financial benefits from legalized gambling, many people oppose opening Maryland to slot machines, anticipating that gambling casinos would follow. "There's no difference between slots and casinos," said Thomas B. Stone, who works for the Restaurant Association of Maryland. Casinos—fairly

# EARNING A LIVING

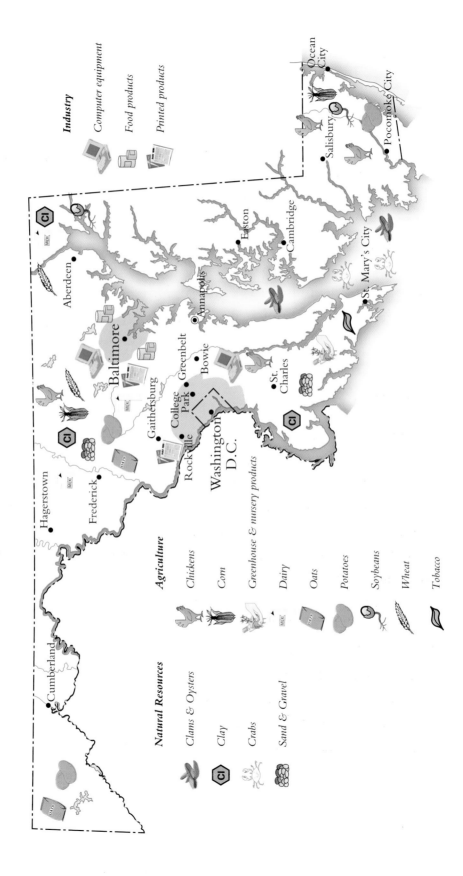

**Industry**

Computer equipment

Food products

Printed products

**Agriculture**

Chickens

Corn

Greenhouse & nursery products

Dairy

Oats

Potatoes

Soybeans

Wheat

Tobacco

**Natural Resources**

Clams & Oysters

Clay

Crabs

Sand & Gravel

Cumberland

Hagerstown

Frederick

Aberdeen

Baltimore

Gaithersburg

Greenbelt

Rockville

College Park

Washington D.C.

Bowie

St. Charles

Annapolis

Easton

Cambridge

St. Mary's City

Salisbury

Ocean City

Pocomoke City

or unfairly—have a reputation for attracting crime and creating seedy neighborhoods.

## MAKING A LIVING

Maryland's economy—like the state itself—is very diverse. This is what you would expect from a state that contains the Chesapeake Bay, farmland, suburban Washington, D.C., and Baltimore—the country's thirteenth-largest city.

Maryland is a technology leader, with several key federal laboratories and agencies located in the state, including the National Institutes for Health, the Goddard Space Flight Center, and the Food and Drug Administration headquarters. High-tech companies, which manufacture electronic components, are attracted to Maryland because they know they will find well-educated, trained workers there.

The service industry is also strong in Maryland, especially in the forty-mile corridor between Baltimore and Washington, D.C. Many Marylanders in the service industry work for government agencies, schools, hospitals, or military bases. Other important service industries are retail sales, insurance, banking, and real estate.

Tourism also plays an important role in Maryland's economy. Thanks to its redeveloped Inner Harbor area, Baltimore now draws almost five million visitors every year. Ocean City, Maryland's largest resort town, attracts more than four million visitors each summer, swelling the town from 7,500 to as many as 300,000 people! Statewide, travel and tourism account for more than 86,000 jobs. Clearly Maryland is happy to welcome visitors—and their wallets.

*Goddard Space Flight Center, Maryland Control Room. Maryland is becoming known as a high-tech area. It ranks sixth in the nation in the number of scientists and engineers per population.*

Western Maryland is a coal-producing region, though the levels of coal mined today don't reach the historic highs of the early 1900s. Marble and limestone are also mined in western Maryland.

The Port of Baltimore is important for shipping. Because the port is farther west than any other major Atlantic seaport, it offers shippers an economical way to transport their goods to the Midwest.

Among Maryland's most important agricultural products are chickens, which are primarily raised on the Eastern Shore, and milk, which is produced in the western part of the state.

Six hundred million chickens are produced annually on Maryland's Eastern Shore.

Farming, including dairy farming, is still an important way of life in Maryland, though more people live in cities than on farms.

## LINKING EAST AND WEST

As early as the 1920s, Maryland's leaders dreamed of connecting the Eastern Shore with the rest of the state by spanning the Chesapeake Bay with a bridge. However, the Great Depression, followed by World War II, delayed any action. In 1947, when the idea of a bridge was brought up again, there was nothing to stop it—except the many people who were opposed to it!

Ferryboat operators knew a bridge would put them out of business. Shipping companies were afraid ships would run into the bridge during foggy weather. And some people on the Eastern Shore just didn't want a bridge, period. There was a tradition against outsiders and change. One group sang, "We don't give a darn for the whole state of Maryland; we're from the Eastern Shore!"

Yet business leaders on the Eastern Shore recognized that a bridge would lead to new markets for farm produce and would attract companies that would create jobs. Ocean City pushed hard for a bridge, because it would bring more tourists to the beaches.

Finally, the bridge was approved. It opened to the public in 1952, and a second span opened in 1973.

Even now, the bridge is breathtaking, its spans gracefully rising 354 feet above the shimmering bay. Perhaps the best way to see the bridge and the bay in all their glory is on foot. One Saturday each May, a span of the bridge is closed to traffic, and thousands of Marylanders stroll the 4.3 miles to the other side as part of the Chesapeake Bay Bridge Walk.

## AN ECONOMY IN TRANSITION

As a colony, Maryland's economy was mainly based on tobacco: "Our meat, drinke, cloathing and monies," said one early Englishman. Early settlers even used tobacco leaves to pay for things before paper money was printed. Though tobacco is still grown in southern Maryland, it is not the economic mainstay it once was, especially as the public keeps insisting on no-smoking zones and state governments sue tobacco companies. "It makes you feel like you're raising an illegal crop," said James Quaide, a tobacco farmer in St. Mary's County. In the 1950s, 5,700 farmers grew more than 40 million pounds of tobacco annually in Maryland. Now, just 1,200 farmers produce about 12 million pounds per year.

*Tobacco was a major export during colonial times. Although it is still grown in southern Maryland, today production is dwindling.*

Government officials have proposed increasing the tax on packs of cigarettes by as much as $1.50. This move is intended to discourage teenagers from smoking, but it would hurt Maryland's tobacco farmers. Even if such measures do not pass, tobacco farmers are not happy. "We're picked on," said Johns Dixon, another St. Mary's tobacco farmer. "There was a time the tobacco farmer was highly respected. Not anymore."

The Chesapeake Bay represents many things to Marylanders, including a source of income. Eastern Shore watermen—and they all seem to be men—sail the bay catching oysters, crabs, and fish that are sold and shipped across the nation. Watermen are proud of their profession; many are following in their fathers' and grandfathers' footsteps. "It's pretty work," said a retired St. Mary's waterman. "I loved the life. I'd rather catch crabs than eat when I'm hungry."

Yet it's getting harder to make a living on the bay. Though the bay provides more than $850 million a year to the shellfish industry in Maryland and Virginia, pollution and overharvesting—catching too many shellfish and fish—have taken their toll. Commercial shad fishing was banned in 1980. Catching striped bass was outlawed for five years, beginning in 1985.

Oyster stocks in the bay have declined to less than 1 percent of what they were in the late 1800s, and pollution and disease in the 1980s further destroyed the oyster population. "Many people around here made their living from these fish," said Denny Bradshaw, a waterman from Smith Island. "Without them there is not much for us to do. People are finding they have to leave [Smith Island] just to make a living."

*Watermen call a big catch of oysters a "jag."*

Even with Maryland's strict regulations on the number and type of oysters watermen can harvest, many people remain concerned about the long-term future of this industry. "We grouse all the time about these restrictions," said Jack Russell, another waterman. "But in the end we're grateful for them. Without them we'd probably take away every oyster in the bay."

Many watermen have begun relying more on crabs. There is a perception that crabs will always be plentiful: "Crabs is like flies. You don't know where they come from, or where they go to, but they always come around," said a seafood packer. Many watermen have doubled or even tripled the number of pots they set out for crabs. Only time will tell whether the bay's crab population can withstand such intense harvesting, and whether proposals to regulate the crab harvest will take effect.

# 4 DIVERSE PEOPLE

**M**aryland was founded as a colony of tolerance, and this legacy is still alive today. Certainly Maryland is not problem-free, but overall, Marylanders today work hard to understand and accept others—just as Lord Baltimore had hoped.

## ETHNIC GROUPS

Before the Civil War, Maryland had the highest population of free blacks of any state in the country. Religious and moral pressures had led many slave owners either to free their slaves outright or to grant them freedom in their wills.

In 1790, only one in thirteen blacks in Maryland was free. By 1810, that figure had risen to one in three. And the 1860 census counted 84,000 "free people of color" in Maryland, 25,000 more than the next highest state. Free blacks lived primarily in Baltimore and the Eastern Shore, building their own communities and working in a variety of jobs, including farming, blacksmithing, and shopkeeping.

Today, about 25 percent of the state's total population is African American. Prince Georges County, just outside Washington, D.C., attracts many highly educated African-American professionals who wish to live in neighborhoods with other successful African Americans. Fifty-seven percent of the county's residents are African

*Many African Americans have moved to Prince Georges County. Of all Maryland counties, it has the highest percentage of its workforce employed in nearby Washington, D.C.*

American, and more than 30 percent of its businesses are owned by African Americans. Clif Webb likes living in there, saying, "Prince Georges County has such a rich cultural and economic diversity that anyone's opportunities are only limited by his or her imagination."

Large numbers of Asians and Latinos also call Maryland home, as do a few thousand American Indians. There are even settlements of Amish, a religious group of farming people who do not rely on modern conveniences such as electricity.

Historically, Baltimore's Locust Point was second only to New York's Ellis Island as a point of entry for people coming by boat to the United States. Thousands of Irish people came to Maryland in the 1830s and 1840s, many of them to work on the Chesapeake and Ohio Canal. The 1850s brought coal miners from Wales. Thousands of Germans, Poles, Russians, and Italians also arrived during the 1800s. By 1870, one of every ten Marylanders was foreign-born.

Baltimore has been called a city of neighborhoods because its nineteenth-century European immigrants tended to live near people from the same country, so they could speak their native language, easily find the kind of food they longed for, and help each other get jobs. Today, many of these neighborhoods maintain their ethnic flavor. "Fells Point is where I buy all my Polish kielbasa," says

**ETHNIC MARYLAND**

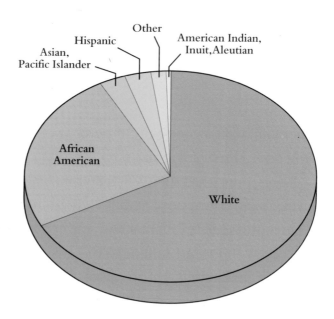

*Baltimore's popular ethnic festivals are a fun way to learn about the foods and customs of different cultures and peoples.*

one suburban woman. "The Polish butcher shops are the best."

Baltimore celebrates its ethnic diversity with summer festivals that attract crowds seeking good food, music, and crafts. Among the heritages celebrated are Greek, Irish, Ukrainian, German, and Polish. "I've been to the Polish festival at Patterson Park," said

Baltimorean Melissa Berg. "It's a big outdoor party: polka bands and accordions, food you can't get anywhere else like three different versions of *bigos* [a stew, sometimes called the Polish national dish], breathtaking dancing. I'm proof that you don't have to be Polish to have fun at the festival!"

Maryland's recent immigrants are even more diverse. One poll found that they come from 145 different countries. Many recent immigrants also live clustered together in ethnic neighborhoods. "Lots of my neighbors are Filipino," said Veronica Puno, who moved from the Philippines to Prince Georges County. "And most of the people who go to my church. As much as we like it here in Maryland, we like to get together to talk about what's going on back 'home.'"

## FINDING SOLUTIONS

Five million people live in Maryland. That's a lot of people for such a small state. In Maryland, an average of 489.2 people live in each square mile, compared to 70.3 for the United States as a whole. If you think that means a lot of people live in cities, you're absolutely right.

Much of Maryland is urban. Almost half the state's residents live in the metropolitan Baltimore area, and one-third live in suburban Washington, D.C. Western Maryland and the Eastern Shore are much less populated, though more people are moving

*Maryland draws immigrants from all over the world. Montgomery County has the highest percentage of foreign-born residents in the state.*

to the counties near the bay, hoping to escape crowds and bad traffic and the general woes of urban living.

The city of Baltimore has lost population in recent decades, as people moved to the suburbs and the less urban counties. In 1950, Baltimore had 950,000 residents—71 percent of the people in the suburban Baltimore region. Now, however, with only 700,000 residents, just 28 percent of the region's 2.5 million residents live in Baltimore.

These changes mean problems for the city. The people who move out of Baltimore tend to be more affluent, so it's the poorer people who are left behind. These people are unable to pay the same amount of taxes that the richer residents did, so it is more difficult for the city to pay for services such as police and fire departments and public schools. To compensate for this loss of tax revenue, business taxes become higher—which sometimes means that businesses don't want to be located in the city, either.

Both the local and state governments are working on innovative ways to solve these problems. By expanding the Baltimore Convention Center, the city hopes to attract more visitors and raise money that way. Additionally, Baltimore has special "enterprise zones." Companies buying new properties or expanding their facilities in these areas receive enormous property tax benefits and other incentives. One local businesswoman said, "These zones help keep companies from moving out of Baltimore—taking jobs with them. Instead, they're willing to invest in property improvements and create jobs."

Too few people is a problem, but so is too many people. Maryland's small towns and rural areas want to retain their charm while

*Small towns are a vital part of Maryland's charm.*

also taking advantage of economic opportunities that might bring in more people. "All of a sudden, everyone in this county seems to want to build a million houses," said Peggy Owens, a native of St. Mary's County in southern Maryland. "The good thing about living here was it was peaceful, quiet. You didn't have to worry about congestion and crime. Now, it's turning into a city, instead of country."

## LIFE ON THE EASTERN SHORE

Novelist Sophie Kerr once said, "If you have not had the luck to be born on the Eastern Shore you cannot know its people." The

Eastern Shore is different from the rest of Maryland. Until the Chesapeake Bay Bridge was completed in 1952, the Eastern Shore was virtually inaccessible. People had to take ferries or drive all the way up around the bay to get there. Residents of the Eastern Shore felt isolated from the rest of the state. In fact, the Eastern Shore tried five times to become its own state, separate from the rest of Maryland, most recently in the 1950s.

The Eastern Shore is home to a special type of Marylander: the waterman. Watermen make their living off the Chesapeake Bay, catching crabs, oysters, clams, and fish. They are only allowed to use boats powered by wind when they go out to work. The boats

*Maryland's Eastern Shore feels and even looks different from other parts of the state. Eastern Shore natives call a person not born on the shore a "Come Here."*

# A WATERMAN'S TALL TALE

Here's a well-known tale told by watermen on the Eastern Shore:

Two Eastern Shore boys, Len and Ward, wanted to command their own ship. They'd been trained by one of the best watermen, Captain Tawes. But they were told, "You're too young. You can take the ship if Captain Tawes goes along too."

The boys begged Captain Tawes to come with them, and finally he agreed.

The three sailed down to the West Indies to load up fruit to bring back to Baltimore. The trip was going well until they got back to the bay and the fog set in so bad that every other ship anchored. But Len and Ward couldn't wait—it was a three-day fog for sure, and they didn't want the fruit to rot. Captain Tawes said, "We can do it, boys. Just bring me a sample from the bottom every half-hour." Watermen claim they can tell exactly where they are by smelling the mud from the bottom of the bay.

So Len brought the first reading to Captain Tawes. He sniffed the mud and said, "Change your course about three points to the westward and that'll put you right in the middle of the channel."

Half an hour later, they brought more mud to Captain Tawes. He said, "Hold right on that course for the next half hour."

Back on deck, Ward said, "Does that old man know what he's saying?"

"Let's see," Len said.

They took dirt from a flowerpot that Len's mother, Betsy, had given him. They dunked the dirt in bay water, and Len took it down to Captain Tawes.

Captain Tawes looked at the mud, smelled it, looked again. "Quick, run tell Ward to heave her hard to. You've run her right in the middle of Betsy's flower garden!"

they use, called skipjacks, have one mast with triangular sails and a shallow V-shaped bottom.

Their work is demanding and dangerous, with the constant risk of getting caught in a storm and drowning. Watermen go out in all sorts of weather—hot, cold, rainy, windy—and because they work for themselves, selling their catch to seafood distributors, there are no paid holidays or paid vacations for watermen.

Yet many watermen wouldn't dream of doing anything else. "When you're getting the oysters and the boat's going good and you've got a good crew, there's nothing like it," said waterman Wade Murphy. "You're out on the bay, and you're part of it."

Eastern Shore writer Gilbert Byron captured the watermen in his poem "These Chesapeake Men":

> These men a sun-tanned, quiet breed
> With eyes of English blue and faces
> Lined with many a watch of sunlit waters . . .
> They seek the imperial shad and the lowly crab,
> The oyster, the weakfish, the turtle, the rockfish, . . .
>
> And food for their souls
> Which they sometimes find . . .
> In the setting of the sun
> In the quest of quiet harbor—
> In the Chesapeake.

## LEISURE

Maryland has been called the Land of Pleasant Living, and Marylanders do their best to uphold that reputation. Hunting is popular;

*The Chesapeake Bay retriever is Maryland's state dog.*

traditionally Maryland was known for its fine duck hunting and the famous Chesapeake Bay retrievers (the state dog), which fearlessly retrieved the catch.

Professional sports occupy many Marylanders' time. In 1984, Baltimoreans were devastated when owner Robert Irsay secretly moved the beloved Baltimore Colts football team to Indianapolis in the dead of night. Ten years later, Bill Gildea wrote, "Even now in Baltimore a melancholy endures." In 1996, the Ravens came to Baltimore, so the town has a new football team to root for. Baseball is big in Maryland. Almost every Baltimore Orioles home game sells out.

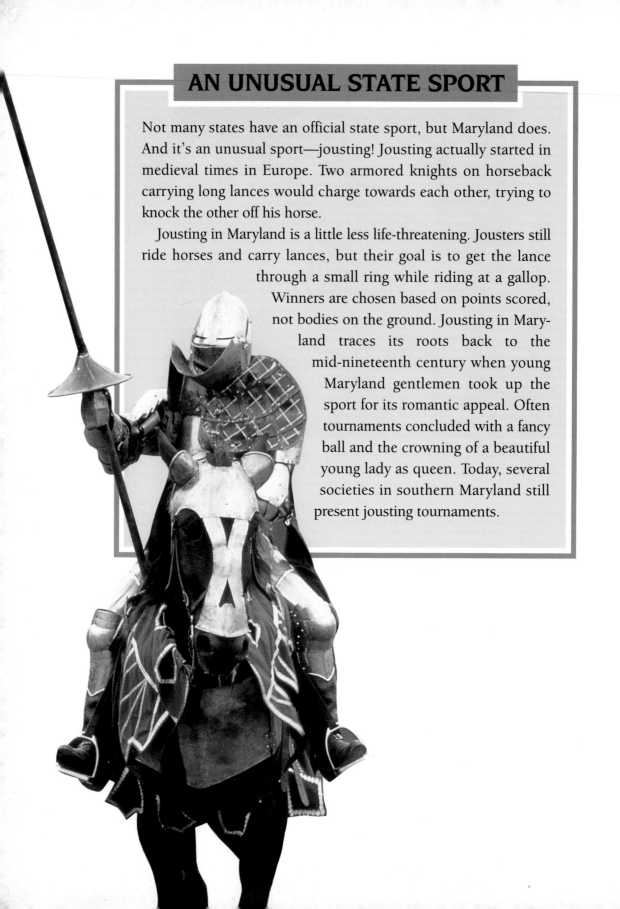

# AN UNUSUAL STATE SPORT

Not many states have an official state sport, but Maryland does. And it's an unusual sport—jousting! Jousting actually started in medieval times in Europe. Two armored knights on horseback carrying long lances would charge towards each other, trying to knock the other off his horse.

Jousting in Maryland is a little less life-threatening. Jousters still ride horses and carry lances, but their goal is to get the lance through a small ring while riding at a gallop. Winners are chosen based on points scored, not bodies on the ground. Jousting in Maryland traces its roots back to the mid-nineteenth century when young Maryland gentlemen took up the sport for its romantic appeal. Often tournaments concluded with a fancy ball and the crowning of a beautiful young lady as queen. Today, several societies in southern Maryland still present jousting tournaments.

# CRABCAKES

There are as many recipes for crabcakes as there are Marylanders. For a real Maryland flavor, add a pinch of Old Bay seasoning to the mayonnaise. Have an adult help you with this recipe:

1 pound lump crabmeat
1 cup crushed saltine crackers
½ cup mayonnaise
1 egg
1 tablespoon mustard
1 tablespoon Worcestershire sauce
Tabasco sauce to taste

Preheat broiler.

Spread the crabmeat out in a flat pan and sprinkle the crushed saltines over it.

In a small bowl, mix the mayonnaise, egg, mustard, Worcestershire sauce, and Tabasco sauce. Pour this mixture over the crabmeat and gently mix together with your hands. Let the mixture sit 2–3 minutes before forming the crabcakes.

Form the mixture into 8 mounded rounds about 3 inches across and 1 inch thick. Do not pack the crab too firmly—just enough to hold the shape.

Arrange crabcakes on a buttered cookie sheet and broil until heated through and slightly browned (about 5–6 minutes). Place aluminum foil over crabcakes if they are browning too quickly.

Serve immediately.

*Marylanders love blue crabs—the freshest are the ones you catch yourself!*

College sports have many fans, too, particularly lacrosse, a Native American game that became popular in Maryland in the late 1800s. Lacrosse is played outdoors. Two teams use netted sticks to throw a ball into a goal. The strategies used are similar to soccer and ice hockey. Johns Hopkins University and the University of Maryland often have nationally ranked teams.

Many Marylanders head for the water whenever they get the chance. They enjoy boating, swimming, beachcombing, and fishing.

Watermen call weekend crabbers "chicken neckers" after the bait they use.

What better way to celebrate your catch than getting together with friends and family for a crab feast? Put brown paper on the picnic table, grab a mallet or knife, and get busy. You'll work just as hard if you go out to eat. William W. Warner described the scene at a crabhouse: "Customers spend an average of four minutes and thirty seconds of do-it-yourself surgery on each crab and get about two ounces of meat per crab for their troubles."

Whether crabbing or cheering on the Orioles or enjoying a kielbasa, Marylanders make the most of what their state offers.

*A summer crab feast. Marylanders may debate the best way to crack open crabs—mallet? knife?—but few debate the delicious results.*

# 5 MARYLAND'S LEADERS

**M**aryland's diversity is reflected in its citizens' accomplishments. From the arts to sports to social reform, Marylanders lead the way.

## STORYTELLERS

Though Edgar Allan Poe was born in Boston, Massachusetts, Maryland stakes a claim to the man who invented the modern detective story. Poe lived in Baltimore from 1831 to 1834, and during this time he published the first of his spine-tingling short stories. Among his best-known works are "The Tell-Tale Heart" and "The Murders in the Rue Morgue."

In 1849, Poe died while passing through Baltimore. He is buried in Westminster Cemetery and Burying Ground in Baltimore. In the early morning hours each year on January 19, Poe's birthday, a mysterious cloaked figure appears and places a half-full bottle of cognac and three roses on Poe's headstone before melting back into the night.

Was Frederick Douglass a writer or a social reformer? This gifted Marylander was both. Born a slave in 1817 on the Eastern Shore, Douglass secretly learned to read when he was a child. At the time, it was illegal to educate slaves in Maryland. Douglass spent his early life working as a field hand on a tobacco plantation before

*Edgar Allan Poe, the author of many chilling stories, died in Baltimore.*

*Frederick Douglass, one of the most important men in the American antislavery movement. Slaves were not supposed to learn how to read, but he managed to teach himself: "I used to carry almost constantly, a copy of Webster's spelling book in my pocket."*

being sent to Baltimore. In his early twenties, he escaped to the North, where he spoke out against the evils of slavery. His first autobiographical book, *Narrative of the Life of Frederick Douglass*, was published in 1845. This powerful account of the horrors of slavery opened many people's eyes to the need to end the inhumane practice.

After the Civil War and the end of slavery, Frederick Douglass wrote: "I felt I had reached the end of the noblest and best part of my life." He remained a champion of African-American rights and also supported the cause of women's rights.

One of Baltimore's most famous sons was H. L. Mencken, a social critic who wrote columns for the *Baltimore Sun* newspaper in the 1920s and 1930s. Mencken used his biting wit to criticize the things he hated most about society: middle-class American life,

*H. L. Mencken, a controversial writer known as the Sage of Baltimore.*

big business, and organized religion. One of his biographers called him "Disturber of the Peace" because of his tendency to rouse people's emotions. A minister upset by Mencken's columns wrote, "That he lives in Baltimore is to Baltimore's disgrace." Mencken also made fun of himself: "The older I grow the more I distrust the familiar doctrine that age brings wisdom."

Baltimorean Barry Levinson is a different type of storyteller. He has written and directed movies about his hometown that capture the quirks and charm of Baltimore. In *Diner*, a group of friends in 1959 try to come to terms with the fact that they're growing up. In one especially memorable scene, a character refuses to marry his fiancée unless she passes a difficult trivia quiz about the Baltimore Colts football team. Newspaper columnist Michael Olesker wrote, "In places around America, audiences laughed at the crazy thought.

*Film director Barry Levinson often sets movies in his native Baltimore.*

*Jazz singer Billie Holiday had her own way of making a sad song come alive. "The pain is etched in her voice," one fan noted.*

People in Baltimore didn't laugh. It seemed perfectly reasonable. Who could marry somebody who didn't know [star quarterback] John Unitas's jersey number?"

Another way of telling a story is through an expressive voice. Billie Holiday is considered the best jazz vocalist of all time. Her style was all her own. She created dramatic effects with unique phrasings, and the power of her personality came through in every song. Holiday, who never received any formal training, was known throughout the country by the time she was twenty. Growing up in Baltimore, she had sung along with records. A friend remembers how "she always like[d] the sad ones." Unfortunately, her life was very sad, as she struggled against heroin addiction, which eventually killed her in 1959.

Grammy Award–winning recording artist Toni Braxton grew up in Severn, Maryland, where she sang in church with her four sisters and won local talent contests. She signed a record deal while she was a student at Bowie State University in Bowie, Maryland. Since the release of her first album, *Toni Braxton*, she has won five Grammy Awards, including Best New Artist in 1993.

*Toni Braxton, the shy minister's daughter who became an international singing star*

## SPORTS

Where would baseball be without the "Sultan of Swat," home-run hitter Babe Ruth? In 1895, George Herman Ruth was born in a brick rowhouse in a working-class South Baltimore neighborhood. "It was a rough, tough neighborhood, but I liked it," Ruth once said. By the time he was seven, he was running wild in the streets, and the courts committed him to Saint Mary's Industrial School for Boys. There, he became a good baseball player. He started as a catcher, but moved to pitcher after filling in for the injured starting pitcher and allowing no hits.

Eventually, Ruth began pitching for the Baltimore Orioles. He got

*Baseball hero Babe Ruth, lower right, started his career as a pitcher but became famous as a slugger.*

his nickname during spring training. According to Ruth, "[Team Manager] Dunn practically led me by the hand from the dressing room to the pitcher's box. I was as proud of my Orioles' uniform as I had been of my first long pants. . . . 'Look at Dunnie and his new Babe,' one of the older players yelled." Ruth later played for the Boston Red Sox and in 1920 was sold to the New York Yankees for the then unheard of sum of $125,000.

Ruth became a larger-than-life baseball hero, winning four World Series with the Yankees and setting many records, including 714 career home runs, a record that wasn't broken until 1974.

A baseball record that isn't likely to be broken for a long, long time is Baltimore Oriole Cal Ripken Jr.'s streak of 2,632 consecutive games played. When New York Yankee Lou Gehrig had set the record of 2,130 baseball games played in a row in 1939, everyone was certain that the record would last forever, but Cal proved them wrong.

Cal Ripken was born in Havre de Grace, Maryland. His father, Cal Sr., worked for the Orioles ball club, and Cal Jr. knew he wanted to be an Oriole. "He lived for the game and to be an Oriole," said his brother Fred.

Cal Jr. made his professional debut in 1981, but the streak didn't actually begin until May 30, 1982. Then Ripken just kept playing—all the way until September 1998, three years after he broke Gehrig's record.

Ripken has led the Orioles to a World Series championship, earned the league's Most Valuable Player Award twice, was selected the 1991 All-Star Game's Most Valuable Player, won two Gold Gloves for his fine fielding at the demanding position of shortstop,

Sometimes a baseball game is more than just a game. All of Maryland beamed with pride when local hero Cal Ripken Jr. broke the record for consecutive games played. That day it seemed as if all of Baltimore was at Oriole Park in Camden Yards.

"Crowds were everywhere starting about noon," said Baltimorean Stan Grubowski. "People without tickets to the game came down just so they could tell their grandkids they were there." Souvenir stands did a brisk business, and the lines to purchase special programs stretched to hundreds of people long.

"We all knew we were going to see a once-in-a-lifetime thing," Grubowski said. The ovations were long and loud any time Ripken was mentioned. It seemed that almost everyone brought a camera; thousands flashed at Ripken's first pitch and any time the ball went to him in the field.

At the end of the fifth inning it was official: Ripken had played in his 2131st game in a row, a monumental achievement. The air filled with confetti and the applause lasted more than twenty minutes, as Ripken ran around the edge of the field, high-fiving with fans. "Big tough men who looked like they chewed nails for a living were standing there with tears rolling down their faces," Grubowski said. "That's one night I'll never forget."

*Gymnast Dominique Dawes shows grace under pressure.*

supports the community through extensive charity work, and still manages to sign autographs for his many fans after games. It seems nothing will stop Cal. He once said, "I don't know if I could put my approach into words; but if I did, I'm sure it would sound like my dad's, something like 'Nothing's worth doing halfway.' I heard my dad say those words, and I witnessed him living his life by them."

Dominique Dawes, one of the first African Americans on the U.S. women's gymnastics team, grew up in Silver Spring, Maryland, and still lives and trains in the area. Among "Awesome Dawesome's" many achievements are a team gold medal and a bronze medal for floor exercise from the 1996 Olympic Games in Atlanta. This well-balanced Marylander was also on her high school honor roll and was elected prom queen.

## SOCIAL REFORMERS

Some Marylanders made contributions that benefited people all across the country. Often change can only come when strong individuals challenge the way things are.

Thurgood Marshall, the first African American to serve on the U.S. Supreme Court, grew up in West Baltimore in the early 1900s. Once, when he misbehaved in school, the principal sent him out of the room until he'd learned a passage from the U.S. Constitution. Eventually Marshall knew the whole Constitution, and he noticed that although the Fourteenth Amendment promised equal rights for everyone, his own experience as a black man showed that was not the case. For example, African-American children were sent to different, worse schools than white children. Eventually, Marshall went to law school at Howard University where teachers encouraged him to make a difference in the world by challenging laws that allowed segregation.

In 1934, a year after he had graduated at the top of his law school class, the National Association for the Advancement of Colored People (NAACP) asked Marshall to help them fight to end racial discrimination. Marshall was proud to join their worthy battle.

Marshall's most important case, *Brown v. Board of Education of Topeka, Kansas*, was decided in 1954. African-American parents were suing the school board so their children could attend public schools that were not segregated by race. Marshall argued this case .

*Thurgood Marshall helped end racial segregation in schools and went on to become the first African-American Supreme Court justice.*

in front of the U.S. Supreme Court, and the justices decided unanimously that segregation in schools was unconstitutional. That was one of the first big steps in the civil rights movement of the 1950s and 1960s. "Because of my participation, I perhaps could overestimate *Brown's* importance," Marshall said later in his life. "I doubt it though."

*Rachel Carson, scientist and author, alerted people to the dangers of pesticides.*

Biologist Rachel Carson has made important contributions to the health of the earth. Carson, who was born in Pennsylvania, attended Johns Hopkins University in Baltimore and spent her later life in Silver Spring, Maryland. Gradually, she became more and more concerned that the pesticides used to kill insects were, in fact, poisoning the earth. "The more I learned about the use of pesticides, the more appalled I became," she said. "Can anyone believe it is possible to lay down such . . . poisons on the earth without making it unfit for all life?" In 1962, Carson published her pathbreaking book, *Silent Spring*.

As a result of *Silent Spring*, the pesticide DDT was banned in this country, the U.S. Congress created the Environmental Protection Agency, and many people leapt into action to try to preserve and protect our fragile planet.

# 6 MARYLAND'S TREASURES

**M**aryland is a small state, but don't for a minute think that means there's little to see or do. On the contrary, Maryland is chock-full of exciting places to visit, ranging from the mountains to the ocean, the city to the country, the glamorous to the simple, and the old to the new. Let's see what the Old Line State holds in store for visitors.

## SWITZERLAND OF AMERICA

With its mountains and twisting trails and waterfalls, western Maryland still has a feeling of wildness about it. In the mid-1800s, this part of Maryland was known as the Switzerland of America because of its picturesque mountains.

People take advantage of western Maryland's beautiful landscape to pursue outdoor activities. The state's largest lake, the man-made Deep Creek Lake, offers boating, swimming, and fishing. Some people even scuba dive, searching for relics from the farmhouses that were submerged when the lake was created in the 1920s. Thousands of homes and cottages line the shore. "It's a great place to go in the summer when you want to beat the heat," says Marylander Cecilia Sager.

Wherever you are in Maryland, you're never more than a few minutes away from a state park or forest. The state owns more than

*City dwellers are drawn to the beautiful wilderness of western Maryland. Garrett County is often called Maryland's Last Frontier.*

280,000 acres of forests, fields, marshes, lakes, rivers, and beaches. The first state forest was set aside in 1906 at Swallow Falls, a beautiful cascade of water that attracts hikers.

Where there are mountains . . . there's skiing! Wisp Resort offers downhill skiing December to mid-March. There are also ample state parks where the less adventurous can enjoy cross-country skiing.

Antietam National Battlefield, near Sharpsburg, was the site of the bloodiest battle of the Civil War. On September 17, 1862, more than 23,000 soldiers were killed there as Confederate forces tried to drive the war northward. Union general Joseph Hooker wrote of the battle, "The slain lay in rows precisely as they had stood in their ranks a few moments before." Today, the peaceful, green park has replaced the scene of destruction. Visitors to the battlefield can trace the phases of the battle, stopping at such spots as Burnside Bridge, where a few Georgia riflemen held off Union soldiers for most of the day, and Bloody Lane, the site of a four-hour battle that resulted in four thousand deaths. A visit to the cemetery is a

*Today, serene Antietam National Battlefield belies its terrifying history as the site of the bloodiest day of the Civil War.*

sobering experience. The visitors center features an audiovisual presentation that provides perspective and background on the battle.

Nearby is the only surviving stone fortification from the French and Indian War. Fort Frederick, built in 1756, is considered the best-preserved Revolutionary stone fort in the country.

## CENTRAL MARYLAND

Visitors to Central Maryland will be surprised at the variety of attractions. Much of this area is farmland, with rolling hills of horse farms, quiet towns, and back roads where you can still find a covered bridge. But this region is also home to the thriving city of Baltimore and the state capital of Annapolis.

**Baltimore: Charm City.** Baltimore, Maryland's biggest city, has reinvented itself as a tourist destination during the past twenty-five years by rebuilding the downtown waterfront into a series of shops, restaurants, and museums called Harborplace. The National Aquarium features dolphin shows, shark feedings, and educational displays about marine life. From the observation deck on the twenty-seventh floor of the World Trade Center, you can look out over the city and beyond to the Chesapeake Bay. Another Harborplace highlight is the U.S. frigate *Constellation*, a ship built in 1797 that was used through the War of 1812, the Civil War, and World War II before being retired.

From Harborplace, tourists can take a water taxi to destinations throughout the city. The funky neighborhood of Fells Point features historic houses, shops, restaurants, and the Broadway Market, which is known for its Polish food stand and butcher shop. The

# PLACES TO SEE

*National Aquarium*

*Harborplace*

*The Maryland Science Center*

*Fort McHenry National Monument*

*Concord Point Lighthouse*

Aberdeen

Baltimore

Hagerstown

Frederick

*Monocacy R.*

*Antietam National Battlefield*

Cumberland

*Potomac R.*

*N. Br. Potomac R.*

*Potomac R.*

Rockville

Gaithersburg

College Park

Greenbelt

Bowie

*NASA/Goddard Visitor Center and Museum*

Washington D.C.

*Potomac R.*

St. Charles

*Calvert Cliffs State Park*

*Patuxent R.*

U.S. Naval Academy

Annapolis

Chesapeake Bay

Easton

Cambridge

*Blackwater National Wildlife Refuge*

*Chesapeake Bay Maritime Museum*

Salisbury

Pocomoke City

Ocean City

*Assateague Island National Seashore*

St. Mary's City Historic

*Calvert Marine Museum*

*Drum Point Lighthouse*

# AND THEY'RE OFF!

Baltimore's Pimlico Race Course is the site of one of the most important horse races in the United States: the Preakness Stakes, held each May. This race is part of the Triple Crown (along with the Kentucky Derby and the Belmont Stakes). A horse that wins all three is declared a Triple Crown Winner—a high honor indeed.

The Preakness started in 1873, two years before the Kentucky Derby. The first race drew seven starters and about 12,000 spectators. Now nearly 100,000 people come to watch the horses run the mile and a half race. "It's like crabs and the Orioles," said Matt Reitter, a university student transplanted from New Jersey. "Everyone said, 'You gotta come out and see it.'"

After the winner has been officially declared, a painter climbs a ladder to the top of a replica of the Old Clubhouse Cupola in the winner's circle. There's a weathervane of a horse and jockey on the cupola, and the painter paints the colors of the new winner's silks on the jockey and horse as everyone cheers.

One official painter said, "It is just the thrill of being able to participate in a big local and national event like this. Let's face it, it's the only televised painting job in the country."

*Visitors can tour Baltimore's Fort McHenry. Francis Scott Key wrote "The Star-Spangled Banner" while watching the British bomb the fort during the War of 1812.*

Baltimore Museum of Industry traces the city's roots as a port city and industrial leader. The Maryland Science Center has live science demonstrations and three floors of hands-on exhibits. The childhood home of Babe Ruth, one of baseball's greatest players, has been restored. Exhibits include rare photos, baseball memorabilia, and game highlights. The B&O Railroad Museum exhibits more than 120 pieces of full-size equipment, including steam, diesel, and electric locomotives and a large collection of railroad artifacts. Fort

McHenry houses exhibits about the War of 1812, when a flag flying high above the fort inspired Francis Scott Key to write "The Star-Spangled Banner."

"There's so much more to Baltimore than you'd expect," said resident Kristy Doty. "No wonder they call it Charm City!"

**Annapolis.** The state house in Annapolis is the oldest continuously operating state capitol in the country. Annapolis, chartered in 1708, is one of the country's oldest cities. Tourists flock to Annapolis to stroll along its picturesque brick streets, stopping at antique shops, restored historic houses, restaurants, and boutiques. No walk through Annapolis is complete without pausing a few moments at the waterfront to watch the parade of boats pass through. "We call it 'Ego Alley' because there's a lot of showing off," said one Annapolis resident.

Annapolis is also home to the U.S. Naval Academy, which was established in 1845. While touring its buildings and grounds, you may catch sight of a traditional wedding at the chapel, where midshipmen create a saber arch for the newly married couple to pass under. Naval Academy graduate Major John Scanlan of the U.S. Marine Corps says, "The last guy in the line taps the bride with his saber and says, 'Welcome to the navy!'"

While Annapolis holds many festivals, one of the most popular is the Kunta Kinte Heritage Festival. This celebration honors the slave whose story Alex Haley told in his best-selling book *Roots*. A plaque near the city dock commemorates the spot where Haley's ancestor came ashore off the slave ship that brought him to America in 1767. The festival includes storytelling, costumed African dancers, and special activities for kids, including mask making.

*Graduation at the U.S. Naval Academy in Annapolis. Major John M. Scanlan, U.S. Marine Corps, said, "My education from the Naval Academy has enabled me to go places and see and do things I never dreamed possible."*

There's more to central Maryland than the bustle of city life. The countryside is perfect for bicycling. Ellicott City, founded in 1772, offers visitors a chance to stroll along a main street that looks pretty much as it did in the town's early days. And at Havre de Grace, the climb to the top of Concord Point Lighthouse is rewarded with a stunning view of the Chesapeake's largest tributary, the Susquehanna River.

**Capital Region.** When the new nation needed land to build its capital city of Washington, D.C., Maryland donated seventy square miles. Three of Maryland's counties are considered suburban Washington, and many visitors drawn to the nation's capital also explore this piece of Maryland.

The Chesapeake and Ohio Canal starts in Washington and stretches 184 miles along the Potomac River all the way to Cumberland in western Maryland. Chesapeake and Ohio National Historical Park runs alongside the canal, offering great biking,

*Riding a boat down the Chesapeake and Ohio Canal*

hiking, fishing, and horseback riding. A museum located at Great Falls, a churning stretch of rapids, explains the canal's historical importance and allows visitors the chance to ride on the canal on an authentic mule-driven boat.

Camp David, the president's mountain retreat, is located in the Catoctin Mountains, just a short helicopter ride from the White House. Though uninvited visitors definitely are not welcome at Camp David, nearby mountain hiking trails, fishing streams, and campsites offer relaxation to the public.

## SOUTHERN MARYLAND

In southern Maryland, you can visit the site of the state's first permanent European settlement, St. Mary's City. It is now a living museum, where costumed interpreters tell visitors about life in the seventeenth century. The eight-hundred-acre complex includes the Godiah Spray Tobacco Plantation, a working reconstruction of a seventeenth-century tobacco plantation, and the *Maryland Dove*, a replica of one of the ships that brought the original settlers from England.

If St. Mary's City isn't old enough for you, check out Calvert Cliffs State Park and Flag Ponds Nature Park, where visitors hunt for the fossilized remains of giant sharks and other sea creatures that roamed the waters 15 million years ago. The parks offer trails, wetlands boardwalks, and visitors centers with displays about the local wildlife.

Solomons Island is now connected to the mainland by a bridge built on a bed of oyster shells, but it still has the feel of the isolated

*A Chesapeake Bay lighthouse*

fishing village it once was. The town's main attraction is the Calvert Marine Museum, which features displays about boat building, plant and animal life of the Chesapeake Bay, and fossils from Calvert Cliffs. The restored Drum Point Lighthouse is one of only three remaining octagonal cottage-type lights of the forty-five that served the bay at the turn of the century.

## KING OYSTER'S FESTIVAL

St. Mary's County has an unusual claim to fame. It's the site of the National Oyster Shucking Championship, held every October as part of the Oyster Festival. Men and women who make their living shucking, or shelling, oysters—whether for canneries or in restaurants—travel to St. Mary's County to compete for the grand prize—the title of U.S. National Oyster Shucking Champion, and a free trip to the world championship held in Ireland.

The champion is judged on speed and skill; the less pieces of shell the better, and the oyster must be cut completely apart from the shell with the sharp knife. Members of the audience cheer their favorite shucker and eagerly await the end of each round when the shuckers pass their opened oysters to the crowd. "They don't get much fresher than this," said one Marylander with a mouthful.

If raw oysters aren't your thing, there are plenty of other options: fried, scalded, and cooked in stew. The luckiest people are the ones judging the National Oyster Cook-Off, which draws more than four hundred entries from all over the country. And through it all, festival mascot King Oyster roams through the crowds, making sure everyone's having fun and getting enough to eat.

## EASTERN SHORE

Maryland's Eastern Shore is framed by the Chesapeake Bay to the west and the Atlantic Ocean and Delaware to the east. Hardly a forgotten corner of the state, this region is now a popular tourist destination.

Families from throughout the East Coast travel to Ocean City during the summer months. "You feel like you've entered another world once you're over," comments Mike Hansen, who spends many summer weekends there. The town features beaches, water sports, fishing, a fun-filled boardwalk, and what one writer described as waves "like tame elephants." "I've been going to Ocean City every summer since I was three years old," Hansen says. "I'll keep going and probably bring my own kids."

In this part of Maryland, the water is not just for fun. The Eastern Shore is dotted with small towns where families rely on the bay for their living. Home of the Maryland waterman—a proud profession of men who sail the bay for crabs and oysters—the Eastern

*About eight million people a year visit Ocean City, Maryland—most of them in the summer.*

*Riding on a skipjack may be the closest one can come to seeing how watermen live and work.*

Shore offers visitors a view of a way of life that is slowly changing.

Many watermen earn extra money by taking visitors out onto the bay on their skipjacks, sharing stories and tall tales, demonstrating how to dredge for oysters, and offering a brief taste of what must be a hard yet immensely satisfying life on the water.

When you want to learn the difference between a skipjack and a bugeye, there's no better place to go than the Chesapeake Bay Maritime Museum in St. Michaels, a picturesque Eastern Shore town that was a shipbuilding center in the late eighteenth and early nineteenth centuries. The museum exhibits bay craft, guns and decoys, and ship models. (By the way, a bugeye was a boat watermen used for dredging oysters before skipjacks were developed in the 1890s. It was bigger, used sails, and didn't have the distinctive V-shaped bottom of the skipjack.)

Duck hunting is an important part of Maryland's heritage, and the carving of duck decoys has evolved into an art form. The decoys at the Ward Museum of Wildfowl Art in Salisbury are so beautiful (and expensive) that no collector would dare put them in the water.

To see the real thing, head to the Blackwater National Wildlife Refuge near Cambridge where migratory waterfowl such as ducks, geese, and swans rest and feed from mid-October to December. The refuge is also home to two endangered species, the bald eagle and the Delmarva fox squirrel.

What makes Maryland truly an exciting state to visit is that all this is just a glimpse of what Maryland offers. There's so much more to see and do!

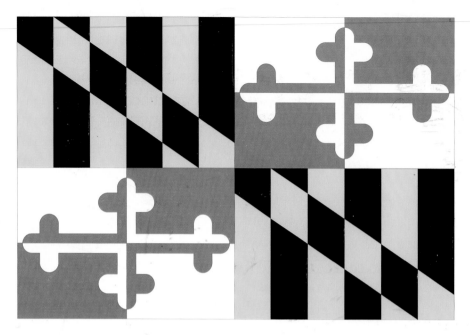

THE FLAG: *The red and white quarters of the flag are the coat of arms of the Crosslands. The black and gold quarters are that of the Calverts.*

THE SEAL: *The front of the state seal shows Lord Baltimore dressed in armor riding a horse along the seashore. On the back a farmer and a fisherman are standing next to a shield bearing the coats of arms of the Calverts and the Crosslands, two branches of Lord Baltimore's family.*

# STATE SURVEY

**Statehood:** April 28, 1788

**Origin of Name:** Named in honor of Queen Henrietta Maria, the wife of the English king Charles I

**Nickname:** Old Line State

**Capital:** Annapolis

**Motto:** Manly Deeds, Womanly Words

**Bird:** Baltimore oriole

**Flower:** Black-eyed Susan

**Tree:** White oak

**Insect:** Baltimore checkerspot butterfly

**Crustacean:** Maryland blue crab

**Dog:** Chesapeake Bay retriever

**Fish:** Rockfish

*Baltimore oriole*

*Black-eyed Susan*

# MARYLAND, MY MARYLAND

James R. Randall, who wrote the lyrics to this song in 1861, hoped that his poem would inspire Maryland to join the Confederacy. Despite the song's great popularity, due in part to its well-known tune, Maryland did not secede. However, 138 years later—in 1939—"Maryland, My Maryland" was adopted as the official state song.

**Words by James R. Randall**

**Music: "Oh, Tannenbaum"**

The des-pot's heel is on thy shore, Mar - y -land, my Mar - y -land! His

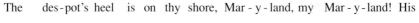

torch is at thy tem-ple door, Mar - y -land, my Mar - y -land! A -

venge the pa - tri - o - tic gore That flecked the streets of Bal - ti - more, And

be the bat - tle queen of yore, Mar - y - land, my Mar - y - land!

**Folk dance:** Square dancing

**Fossil shell:** Ecphora gardnerae

**Sport:** Jousting

## GEOGRAPHY

**Highest Point:** 3,360 feet above sea level, at Backbone Mountain

**Lowest Point:** sea level along the Atlantic coast

**Area:** 10,455 square miles

**Greatest Distance, North to South:** 124 miles

**Greatest Distance, East to West:** 238 miles

**Bordering States:** Pennsylvania to the north, West Virginia to the west, Virginia to the south, Delaware to the east

**Hottest Recorded Temperature:** 109°F in Allegany County on July 3, 1898

**Coldest Recorded Temperature:** -40°F in Oakland on January 13, 1912

**Average Annual Precipitation:** 43 inches

**Major Rivers:** Chester, Gunpowder, Nanticoke, Patapsco, Patuxent, Potomac, Susquehanna, Youghiogheny

**Major Lakes:** Deep Creek, Liberty, Loch Raven, Prettyboy

**Trees:** ash, beech, cypress, hemlock, hickory, maple, oak, red gum, spruce, tupelo

*Woodchuck*

**Wild Plants:** azalea, blackberry, black-eyed Susan, dewberry, laurel, raspberry, rhododendron

**Animals:** chipmunk, cottontail rabbit, gray fox, mink, opossum, otter, raccoon, red fox, squirrel, white-tailed deer, woodchuck

**Birds:** bluebird, cardinal, duck, goose, great blue heron, grouse, mockingbird, partridge, plover, sand-piper, wild turkey, woodcock

**Fish:** bluefish, carp, crab, croaker, sea trout, shrimp, striped bass

**Endangered Animals:** American peregrine falcon, bald eagle, bog turtle, Delmarva Peninsula fox squirrel, dwarf wedge mussel, Indiana bat, Maryland darter, northeastern beach tiger beetle, piping plover, puritan tiger beetle

*Bog turtle*

**Endangered Plants:** Canby's dropwort, harperella, northeastern bulrush, sandplain gerardia, sensitive joint-vetch, swamp pink

# TIMELINE

## Maryland History

**1500s** Choptank, Nanticoke, Patuxent, Piscataway, Pocomoke, Portobago, Wicomico, and Susquehannock Indians live in the region

**1572** Spaniard Pedro Menéndez de Avilés becomes one of the first Europeans to enter the Chesapeake Bay

**1608** John Smith explores the Chesapeake Bay

**1631** William Claiborne establishes a trading post on Kent Island, which is the first European settlement in Maryland

**1632** King Charles I of England grants Lord Baltimore the charter for the Maryland colony

**1634** The first European settlers arrive in Maryland

**1649** Maryland passes a religious toleration act

**1694** The capital moves from St. Mary's to Annapolis

**1727** The *Maryland Gazette*, the first newspaper in the southern colonies, begins publication

**1729** Baltimore is founded

**1767** Charles Mason and Jeremiah Dixon complete their survey of the Maryland-Pennsylvania border, establishing the Mason-Dixon Line

**1775** The American Revolution begins

**1784** The Treaty of Paris ending the American Revolution is signed in Annapolis

1788  Maryland becomes the seventh state

1791  Maryland contributes land for the District of Columbia

1814  Francis Scott Key writes "The Star-Spangled Banner"

1828  Construction begins on the Baltimore and Ohio Railroad

1830  The *Tom Thumb*, the first American steam engine, begins operating between Baltimore and Ellicotts' Mills

1844  The first telegraph line in the U.S. begins operation between Baltimore and Washington, D.C.

1845  The U.S. Naval Academy is founded at Annapolis

1861  The Civil War begins; although Maryland is a slave state, it remains in the Union

1862  The Battle of Antietam is fought in western Maryland

1864  Maryland abolishes slavery

1867  Maryland adopts its fourth and present constitution

1876  Johns Hopkins University opens in Baltimore

1904  A fire destroys downtown Baltimore

1937  The state legislature approves Maryland's first state income tax

1952  The Chesapeake Bay Bridge (later renamed the William P. Lane, Jr., Memorial Bridge) opens, connecting Maryland's Eastern and Western Shores

1954  Baltimore's public schools are desegregated

**1967** Marylander Thurgood Marshall becomes the first African American on the U.S. Supreme Court

**1983** Maryland and neighboring states begin working to clean up the Chesapeake Bay

**1988** Maryland celebrates its 200th birthday

## ECONOMY

**Agricultural Products:** cattle, chickens, corn, greenhouse and nursery plants, milk, soybeans, wheat

**Manufactured Products:** chemicals, electrical equipment, food products, printed materials, steel

**Natural Resources:** clay, crushed stone, fish, sand and gravel

**Business and Trade:** finance, health care, insurance, wholesale and retail trade

*Port of Baltimore*

## CALENDAR OF CELEBRATIONS

**National Outdoor Show** Log-sawing, duck-calling, and trap-setting contests make for a fun February weekend in Golden Hill.

**Maple Syrup Demonstration and Mountain Heritage Festival** Come watch the sap flow in Thurmont. At this March event, you can see tree-tapping and sap-boiling demonstrations and also enjoy storytelling and old-fashioned carriage rides.

**Celtic Festival of Southern Maryland** Each April people in St. Leonard kick up their heels at this celebration of all things Celtic. There's plenty of piping, fiddling, dancing, athletic competitions, food, and crafts from Scotland, Ireland, and Wales.

**Maryland Preakness Celebration** In Baltimore, the Preakness is more than just a horse race. It's also the end of a weeklong May celebration that features hot-air balloon races, parades, and concerts.

**Chesapeake and Ohio Canal Festival** Each May Cumberland commemorates the importance of the canal to nineteenth-century Maryland with a festival that includes rides on a replica of a canal boat, horse-and-buggy rides, an ox roast, and a street dance.

**Montgomery County Ethnic Heritage Festival** At this June event, Silver Spring celebrates the more than 80 different cultures of the people who have settled there. You can sample foods ranging from Thai to Colombian to Australian and play games from around the world. International dancers, musicians, and crafts exhibits are also part of the festivities.

**Cozy's Strawberry Festival** You'll want to be hungry for this festival honoring the strawberry harvest in June in Thurmont. You can enjoy strawberry pies, shakes, shortcake, sundaes, drinks and more. A strawberry-eating contest, folk music, and crafts displays add to the fun.

**Ice Cream Festival** Nearly 10,000 pounds of ice cream are eaten during this three-day July festival in Baltimore. You can eat yours in cones, floats, and sundaes. You can also taste new flavors that ice-cream makers are testing.

**Friendsville Fiddle and Banjo Contest** Every July since 1964, musicians from the Friendsville area have gotten together for a day filled with toe-tapping bluegrass and old-time country music.

**Rocky Gap Country Music Bluegrass Festival** Some of the brightest stars in country music gather in Cumberland each August for a weekend of concerts, workshops, sing-alongs, craft demonstrations, and children's activities.

**Old St. Joseph's Jousting Tournament and Horse Show** Competitors test their skill at Maryland's official state sport at this August event in Easton. Besides watching horsemen try to spear rings, you can also attend a horse show or a medieval pageant and enjoy lots of great food at a country picnic.

**National Hard Crab Derby** Crisfield calls itself the Crab Capital of America, and each September the town stakes its claim to this title by holding the largest seafood festival on the Chesapeake Bay. Events include a crab race, a crab-picking contest, the crowning of Miss Crustacean, and a big fireworks display.

**Polkamotion-by-the-Ocean** Thousands of couples twirl the nights away to the sounds of the nation's best polka bands during this four-day September event in Ocean City.

**St. Mary's County Oyster Festival** The National Oyster Shucking Championship and the National Oyster Cook-Off are the big draws at this October extravaganza in Leonardtown. After you've had your fill of oysters prepared every possible way, you can shop at a flea market, watch a puppet show, or enjoy a hayride.

**German Fest** The emphasis at this October event in Thurmont is on food. You can eat German potato salad, bratwurst, dumplings, and strudel, all while listening to German accordion tunes.

**Waterfowl Festival** Displays of duck decoys, decoy-carving demonstrations, and duck- and goose-calling contests are all part of fun when Easton celebrates the return of thousands of waterfowl for the winter each November.

**Christmas in Annapolis** Annapolis is at its loveliest and most festive during the Christmas season. During December, you can tour exquisitely decorated 18th-century homes, watch a parade of yachts festooned with lights, and join in candlelit caroling.

## STATE STARS

**Benjamin Banneker** (1731–1806), an astronomer, mathematician, and surveyor, was one of the first African-American scientists. The son of a slave who had bought his own freedom, Banneker attended school for several years and then continued to read extensively, teaching himself astronomy. During his varied career, he helped survey and lay out Washington, D.C., and published his own almanac containing astronomical, weather, and tide predictions. Banneker was born in Ellicotts' Mills.

**Eubie Blake** (1883–1983), one of the most gifted ragtime musicians and composers, was born in Baltimore. Blake grew up listening to ragtime's intricate, lively rhythms and began performing professionally as a teenager. He wrote his first important song, "The Charleston Rag," in 1899. Among his other well-known songs is "I'm Just Wild about Harry." In 1978, Blake's life and music were celebrated in a hit Broadway show called *Eubie*.

*Eubie Blake*

**John Wilkes Booth** (1838–1865) was the
assassin of President Abraham Lincoln.
Booth was a well-regarded actor whose
sympathies lay with the South during the
Civil War. He shot Lincoln at Ford's The-
atre in Washington, D.C., and escaped
into Maryland. He was killed a few days
later when he was captured. Booth was
born in Bel Air.

*John Wilkes Booth*

**James M. Cain** (1892–1977) was a master of tough, unsentimental crime
fiction. Cain, who was born in Annapolis, began his career as a journalist
in Baltimore and New York City. He eventually turned his attention to
fiction. His first novel, *The Postman Always Rings Twice*, about a woman
and her lover conspiring to murder her husband, brought him fame.
Many of Cain's novels, such as *Double Indemnity*, are classics of hard-
boiled fiction.

**Rachel Carson** (1907–1964) was a marine biologist and environmental
writer. Carson, who lived in Silver Spring, spent most of her career working for the U.S. Fish and Wildlife Service. She first earned fame for her
book *The Sea Around Us*, about the history and biology of the sea, which
won the National Book Award and sat atop the best-seller list for 39
weeks. She is best remembered for her 1962 book *Silent Spring*, which
warned Americans about the danger of pesticides.

**Tom Clancy** (1947–    ) is the author of many best-selling thrillers. Many
of his books, including *The Hunt for Red October* and *Patriot Games*, have

been made into popular motion pictures. Clancy was born in Baltimore and now lives in Calvert County.

**Frederick Douglass** (1817–1895) was a writer and antislavery activist. Douglass was born a slave in Tuckahoe. He escaped to freedom in 1838 and quickly became a powerful voice in the antislavery movement. During the Civil War, Douglass lobbied President Abraham Lincoln to include African-American soldiers among Union forces, and he later tried to improve their treatment. After the war, he continued to speak out for civil rights and women's rights. He also held various government posts, including minister to Haiti.

**Philip Glass** (1937–    ) is an influential composer, renowned for his trancelike music. Born in Baltimore, Glass was a gifted child. He entered the University of Chicago at age 14 and later studied at New York's Juilliard School of Music. In the 1960s, he traveled to India and Tibet and was influenced by the music there. He began incorporating the rhythms of Eastern music into his work, creating repetitive compositions featuring layers of sound. His most famous work is the opera *Einstein on the Beach*.

**Dashiell Hammett** (1894–1961), a native of St. Mary's County, created "hard-boiled" detective fiction. Previously, mysteries had always featured glamorous detectives, but Hammett's characters were just sloppy men doing an unglamorous job. Later, he created the unforgettable Sam Spade, the original wisecracking tough-guy detective. Hammett's classic novels include *The Maltese Falcon*, *Red Harvest*, and *The Thin Man*.

**Matthew Henson** (1866–1955), an African-American explorer from Charles County, was one of the first two men to reach the North Pole. Henson always had a love of adventure. At thirteen, he took a job on a ship bound

*Matthew Henson*

for China. In 1888, he first worked for explorer Robert Peary. Three years later, they went to Greenland where Henson befriended the Inuit, the native people who lived there, and learned their language. Peary and Henson returned to Greenland time and again in their attempt to reach the North Pole. They finally succeeded in 1909.

**Johns Hopkins** (1795–1873), a merchant, banker, and philanthropist from Anne Arundel County, gave his name to Baltimore's most famous university and hospital. Hopkins's wholesale grocery business in Baltimore had made him rich. He also helped organize the Baltimore and Ohio Railroad. When he died, he left millions of dollars to found Johns Hopkins University and Johns Hopkins Hospital.

**Billie Holiday** (1915–1959) was one of America's greatest jazz singers. From the time she first garnered notice singing in the jazz clubs of Harlem, Holiday stunned audiences. Her unusual phrasing made her songs sad, sensual, and poignant. In 1938, she began singing with Artie Shaw, becoming one of the first African Americans to sing with a white orchestra. In 1974, her autobiography, *Lady Sings the Blues*, was made into a successful film. Holiday was born in Baltimore.

**Francis Scott Key** (1779–1843), who was born in Frederick County, earned his place in history by writing "The Star-Spangled Banner." Key watched the British bombardment of Fort McHenry during the War of 1812. The following morning, when he saw the American flag still flying over the fort,

*Francis Scott Key*

he wrote the words to the song in relief. The poem was soon reprinted in newspapers throughout America, but it did not become the United States' official national anthem until 1931.

**Barry Levinson** (1942–      ), a noted movie director and writer, grew up in Baltimore. His first film, *Diner*, is an affectionate look at growing up in 1950s Baltimore. Later films, such as *Tin Men* and *Avalon*, also have Baltimore settings. In 1988, Levinson's film *Rain Man*, about a brash young man and his autistic brother, won several Academy Awards, including Best Director and Best Picture.

**Thurgood Marshall** (1908–1993), a Baltimore native, was the first African American to sit on the U.S. Supreme Court. During the 1940s and 1950s, he was the nation's preeminent civil rights lawyer, winning 29 of 32 cases that he argued before the Supreme Court. In his most famous case, *Brown v. Board of Education of Topeka, Kansas*, the Court agreed and declared the segregation of public schools illegal. Marshall was appointed to the Supreme Court in 1967 and served until 1991.

**H. L. Mencken** (1880–1956) was a journalist and social critic whose savagely funny columns poked fun at politicians, religion, and middle-class values. Mencken became a reporter for the *Baltimore Morning Herald* at age 18. By age 25, he had become the paper's editor-in-chief. He later moved to the *Baltimore Sun*. Mencken also shaped public opinion and literary tastes as a writer and editor of such sophisticated magazines as *Smart Set* and *American Mercury*. He was born in Baltimore.

**Barbara Mikulski** (1936–      ) was the first female U.S. senator from Maryland, the first Democratic woman to hold a U.S. Senate seat not previously held by her husband, and the first

*Barbara Mikulski*

woman to win a statewide election in Maryland. Mikulski grew up in Baltimore and became a social worker. In 1971, she was elected to the Baltimore City Council. She moved to the U.S. House in 1977 and then to the Senate ten years later. Mikulski is known for her feisty liberal and feminist views.

**Phyllis Reynolds Naylor** (1933–    ) has written many acclaimed books for young people. She is perhaps best known for writing books about serious subjects, such as *The Keeper*, which concerns mental illness. But she has also written lighthearted mysteries, such as *The Agony of Alice*. Her 1992 novel *Shiloh*, about an abused dog, won the prestigious Newbery Award. Naylor lives in Bethesda.

**Charles Willson Peale** (1741–1827), one of the leading American painters of his age, was born in Queen Annes County. Peale, the first painter to do a portrait of George Washington, made his reputation as a portraitist. He established the oldest art school in the country, the Pennsylvania Academy of Fine Arts. He also founded the first scientific museum in the

United States, which housed live reptiles, fish, and toads, along with larger stuffed animals. It even held an entire mastodon skeleton that Peale had helped excavate. His most famous painting, *Exhumation of the Mastodon*, documents this event.

**Adrienne Rich** (1929–    ), a native of Baltimore, is a leading poet, whose work often reflects her commitment to feminism and social change. In bold language, she writes about very specific situations while also

*Charles Willson Peale*

noting how they are part of larger trends in society. Her 1966 collection, *Necessities of Life*, won the National Book Award.

**Cal Ripken Jr.** (1960–     ), of Havre de Grace, is one of the best all-round shortstops in baseball history. Ripken, who has spent his entire career with the Baltimore Orioles, holds the record for the most consecutive games played, at 2,632. He has also won the American League Most Valuable Player Award twice and has more career home runs than any other American League shortstop.

**George Herman "Babe" Ruth** (1895–1948), one of the greatest players in baseball history, was born in Baltimore. For many years he held the record for most home runs in a single season. His record of 714 career home runs stood until 1974. Ruth was one of the first five players elected to the National Baseball Hall of Fame.

**Upton Sinclair** (1878–1968) was a writer and social critic best remembered for his novel *The Jungle*, which exposed the filthy conditions and unfair labor practices in the meat-packing industry. The outcry that resulted from the book provoked the passage of the Pure Food and Drug Law. Sinclair wrote more than 90 other books, which often dealt with corruption and unsafe practices in industry. Sinclair was born in Baltimore.

*Upton Sinclair*

**Harriet Tubman** (1820–1913) was a leading figure in the Underground Railroad, which helped escaped slaves make their way to freedom in the North. Tubman, who was born a slave in Bucktown, escaped north in 1848. During the next ten years, she made many trips south, helping 300 people escape, including her parents. During the Civil War, Tubman worked as a nurse, a spy, and a scout for the Union army. After the war, she worked for women's rights and established a home for elderly and needy African Americans.

**Anne Tyler** (1941–    ), who lives in Baltimore, is an acclaimed novelist. Her works, such as *The Accidental Tourist* and *Dinner at the Homesick Restaurant*, are noted for their mix of comedy and drama. In 1989, her novel *Breathing Lessons* won the Pulitzer Prize in fiction.

**Frank Zappa** (1940–1993) was a groundbreaking rock musician. An accomplished composer, Zappa's songs ranged from jazz to rock to modern classical. He often used montage techniques, interweaving rock and orchestral music with spoken words and bursts of noise. His more than 60 albums, including *We're Only in It for the Money* and *Weasels Ripped My Flesh*, often featured satirical songs with sharp political content. Zappa was born in Baltimore.

*Frank Zappa*

## TOUR THE STATE

**Antietam National Battlefield and Shrine** (Sharpsburg) After touring the bloodiest battlefield of the Civil War and visiting the cemetery where nearly 5,000 soldiers are buried, you can stop at the visitors center and learn about how the battle turned the tide of the war in favor of the Union.

**Western Maryland Scenic Railroad** (Cumberland) This 1916 locomotive takes visitors on a 32-mile trip through the lovely Allegheny Mountains.

**Havre de Grace Decoy Museum** (Havre de Grace) This unusual museum is filled with 1,500 decoys shaped like ducks, geese, and swans. On weekends you can watch craftspeople demonstrate the art of carving decoys.

**Swallow Falls State Park** (Oakland) Trails along the rugged Youghiogheny River take hikers past rocky gorges to a stunning waterfall. The park is also a great place to fish and camp.

*Fort McHenry*

**Fort McHenry National Monument and Shrine** (Baltimore) This star-shaped fort, which was finished in 1803, today looks much like it did during the Civil War. You can tour restored guardrooms and barracks, examine early American weapons, and sometimes even watch reenactments of life at the fort during the 19th century.

**Baltimore Streetcar Museum** (Baltimore) Hop onto a restored streetcar for a 1.25-mile ride into yesteryear. Many other streetcars dating back as far as 1859 are also on display.

**National Aquarium** (Baltimore) More than 5,000 fish, sharks, dolphins, reptiles, birds, and other creatures live at this aquarium, the most visited tourist site in Maryland. Highlights include the coral reef exhibit, the shark tank, and the rain forest exhibit.

**American Visionary Art Museum** (Baltimore) This fascinating museum displays works by artists who taught themselves, including farmers, housewives, the disabled, and the homeless. The paintings and sculptures are sometimes made from unusual materials such as toothpicks and household utensils.

**Babe Ruth Birthplace and Baseball Center** (Baltimore) The man many people believe was the greatest baseball player ever was born in this brick rowhouse. Today the house is filled with photos, film clips, and memorabilia of Ruth and other great Baltimore baseball players.

**Maryland State House** (Annapolis) First occupied in 1780, this is the oldest state capitol to be continuously used as a legislature. The building's intricate woodwork and wooden dome are particularly striking.

**NASA/Goddard Visitor Center and Museum** (Greenbelt) This museum provides visitors with a close-up view of satellites, rockets, and space capsules. You might even see a model rocket launch.

**Spruce Forest Artisan Village** (Grantsville) Potters, weavers, stained-glass makers, and others create their crafts in this village's 19th-century log buildings.

**Calvert Cliffs State Park** (Lusby) More than 600 kinds of fossils, some 15 million years old, have been found embedded in the Calvert Cliffs, which tower above Chesapeake Bay. Visitors can scour the beach looking for shark's teeth and other fossils. Any they find are theirs to keep.

**Historic St. Mary's City** (Lexington Park) You can journey back to colonial times when you visit the site of the first European settlement in Maryland. The museum includes the reconstructed state house, which was first built in 1676, a replica of the *Dove*, a boat that brought the first European settlers to colonial Maryland, and the Godiah Spray Tobacco Plantation, where costumed guides depict life in the 17th century.

**Battle Creek Cypress Swamp Sanctuary** (Prince Frederick) This is the northernmost stand of towering bald cypress trees in the United States. A boardwalk that winds through the swamp gives you a close-up view of the native plants and animals.

**Blackwater National Wildlife Refuge** (Cambridge) Bald eagles, ospreys, Canada geese, peregrine falcons, Delmarva fox squirrels, and many other creatures make their home at this refuge. Hiking trails provide visitors views of the region's woodlands, marshes, ponds, and other habitats.

**Assateague Island National Seashore** (Assateague Island) This pristine island is ideal for camping, hiking, fishing, and picnicking. Keep an eye out for the wild ponies that roam the island.

**Chesapeake Bay Maritime Museum** (St. Michaels) Displays of boats, ranging from skipjacks to Indian dugout canoes, are just one highlight of this museum. There are also exhibits about fishing, navigation, and boat building, an aquarium, and a six-sided lighthouse built in 1879.

**Ward Museum of Wildfowl Art** (Salisbury) The history of decoys is brought to life at this museum. Displays range from replicas of the reed figures Native Americans would have made a thousand years ago to intricate contemporary carvings worth hundreds of thousands of dollars.

## FUN FACTS

Baltimore is the site of the nation's first umbrella factory. The company's slogan was "Born in Baltimore—raised everywhere."

The first practical refrigerator was invented in Baltimore in 1803.

Baltimore is also the site of many other firsts. Peter Cooper built the country's first coal-burning steam engine in 1830 for the Baltimore and Ohio Railroad. The nation's first telegraph began operation in 1844 between Baltimore and Washington, D.C. And the country's first elevated electric railway was built in Baltimore in 1893.

# FIND OUT MORE

If you would like to learn more about Maryland, look for the following titles in your library or bookstore.

## BOOKS

### General State Books

Fradin, Dennis Brindell. *America the Beautiful: Maryland.* New York: Children's Press, 1997.

Thompson, Kathleen. *Maryland.* Austin, TX: Raintree Steck-Vaughn Publishers, 1996.

### Special Interest Books

Fradin, Dennis Brindell. *The Maryland Colony.* Chicago: Children's Press, 1990.

McClard, Megan. *Harriet Tubman: Slavery and the Underground Railroad.* Englewood Cliffs, NJ: Silver Burdett Press, 1991.

Ruckert, Norman G. *Fort McHenry: Home of the Brave.* Baltimore: Bodine & Associates, 1983.

Wilson, Richard, and Jack Bridner. *Maryland: Its Past and Present*. Lanham, MD: Maryland Historical Press, 4th Edition, 1992.

## Novels

Sharpe, Susan. *Waterman's Boy*. New York: Bradbury Press, 1990. A children's novel set on the Eastern Shore.

## CD-ROMS

*State Greats*. Atlanta, GA: Gallopade Publishing Group. Information on fifty important Marylanders.

*State Hard-to-Believe (But True!) History, Mystery, Trivia, Legend, Lore & More*. Atlanta, GA: Gallopade Publishing Group. Interesting tidbits about Maryland.

*State Timelines*. Atlanta, GA: Gallopade Publishing Group. Maryland history.

## WEBSITES

These informative websites can be easily found on the Internet:

http:\\www.gov.state.md.us
   This webpage offers information about Maryland's history and government.

http:\\www.mdisfun.org
   Connected with the state tourism department, this site describes special places and events in Maryland, with a special section for kids.

# INDEX

Page numbers for charts, graphs, and illustrations are in boldface.

military bases, 58
miners, 59, 70
Montgomery County, 72, **73**
motto, 119
mountains, 12, 13–14, 102, 112, 121
movies, 89, 132
Muddy Creek Falls, **16**
Murray, Donald, 46–48
museums, 108–109, 112, 113, 116–117, 136, 137, 138
music, 38, **39**, **90**, 90–91, **91**, 120, 124, 127, 128, 130, 135

NASA Goddard Space Flight Center, 58, **59**, 137
Native Americans, 21, 32–33, 34–35, 69, 82, 123, 138
natural resources, 125
Naylor, Phyllis Reynolds, 133
newspapers, 88, 123, 132
novelists, 75, 109, 129–130, 134

Ocean City, 58, 61, 114–115, **115**
Old Line State, 37
Olesker, Michael, 9, 89–90
oysters, **25**, 29, **47**, 63–64, **64**, 114

parks, **16**, 21, 102–103, 111, 112, 136, 137
Peale, Charles Wilson, 133, **133**
*Pfiesteria piscicida*, 24
Piedmont Plateau, 14–15 40
Pimlico Race Course, **14**, 107, **107**
plantations, 34, 40, 112
plants, 18, 27, 122, 137
Poe, Edgar Allan, 86, **87**
poets, 38–39, **39**, 78, 133–134

Poles, 70–72
pollution, 24, 27–28, 63
ponies, 19, **20**, 138
population, 29, **37**, 43, 48–49, 72, 74–75
  growth, **43**
  largest cities, **48**
Potomac River, **13**, 15, 34
poverty, 48–49, 74
The Preakness, **14**, 107, **107**, 126
Prince Georges County, 68–69, **69**, 72

railroads, 39, 108–109, 124, 131, 135, 138
Randall, James R., 120
recreation, 18, 78–83, 102, 110, 111–112. *see also* sports
religion, 34, 49, 123
restaurants, 9, 49, 83, 105
Revolutionary War, 36–37, 123
Rich, Adrienne, 133–134
Rigby, James H., 42
Ripken, Cal, Jr., 93–95, **94**, 134
rivers, **13**, 15, 18, 20, 24, 32, 34, 110–111, 121
Ruth, Babe, **92**, 92–93, 108, 134, 137

St. Clement's Island, 34, **35**
St. Mary's City, 34, 112, 123, 137
Schmoke, Kurt, **55**
segregation, 96–97, 124, 130, 132. *see also* civil rights
servants, 34
settlers, 20, 34–35, **35**, 123
Sharpsburg, 42, 103
ships. *see* boats
Sinclair, Upton, 134
skiing, 103
skipjacks, **25**, 76–78, **116**
slavery, 34, 40, 41, 68,

86–88, 109, 124, 134. *see also* African Americans
Sluyter, Peter, 20
Smith, John, **17**, 32–33, 123
Smith Island, 63
soldiers, 36–37, 40–42, 43, 130
Solomons Island, 112–113
songs, 44, 61, 120. *see also* music
southern Maryland, 75, 112–113
sports, 79–80, 82, **92**, 92–96, 103
state, 80, **80**
  water, 82, 102
squirrels, 19, **19**
Star-Spangled Banner, 38, **39**, 124
statehood, 119, 124
steam engine, 39, 124, 138
streetcars, 136
Susquehanna River, 18, 20, 32, 110–111

tall tale, 77
taxes, 36, 63, 74, 124
technology, 58, **59**
telegraph, 138
tobacco, 34, 40, 61–63, **62**
*Tom Thumb*, 124
tourism, 24, 58, 74, 105–117, **106**, 135–138, 140
towns, 74–76, **76**, 110–111
transportation, 38–39, 61, 76
Treaty of Paris, 37, 123
trees, 18, 27–28, 121, 137
  state, 119
Tubman, Harriet, 41, **41**, 134–135
Tyler, Anne, 135

Underground Railroad, 41, 134–135
U.S. Naval Academy, 109, **110**, 124

CONFIDENTIAL CONFIDENTIAL CONFIDENTIAL CONFIDENTIAL
CONFIDENTIAL CONFIDENTIAL CONFIDENTIAL CONFIDENTIAL
CONFIDENTIAL CONFIDENTIAL CONFIDENTIAL CONFIDENTIAL
CONFIDENTIAL CONFIDENTIAL CONFIDENTIAL CONFIDENTIAL
CONFIDENTIAL CONFIDENTIAL CONFIDENTIAL CONFIDENTIAL